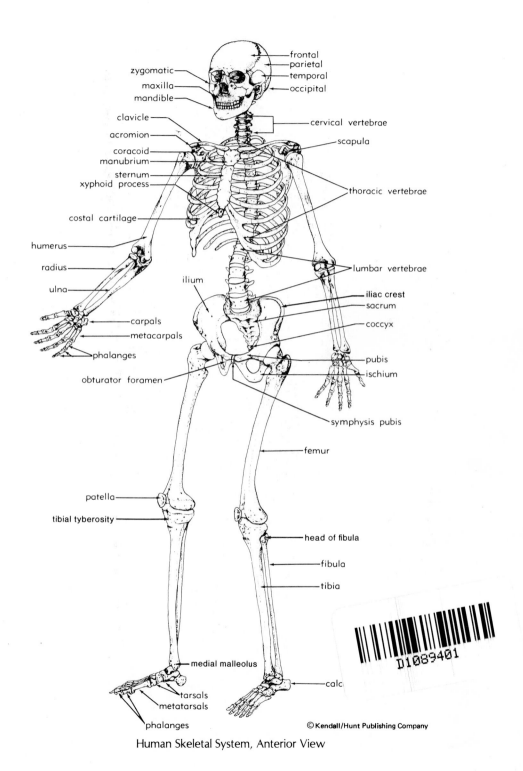

frontal
parietal
temporal
occipital

zygomatic
maxilla
mandible

clavicle
acromion
coracoid
manubrium
sternum
xyphoid process

costal cartilage

humerus

radius

ulna

ilium

carpals
metacarpals

phalanges

obturator foramen

cervical vertebrae

scapula

thoracic vertebrae

lumbar vertebrae

iliac crest
sacrum
coccyx

pubis
ischium

symphysis pubis

femur

patella

tibial tyberosity

head of fibula

fibula

tibia

medial malleolus

calc

tarsals
metatarsals

phalanges

© Kendall/Hunt Publishing Company

Human Skeletal System, Anterior View

PERSONALIZED WEIGHT TRAINING FOR FITNESS AND ATHLETICS

From Theory to Practice
Second Edition

Frederick C. Hatfield, Ph.D.
Muscle & Fitness *Magazine*

March L. Krotee, Ph.D.
University of Minnesota

KENDALL/HUNT PUBLISHING COMPANY
Dubuque, Iowa

B   403219   01

Contents

Foreword

Interest in training with weights has accelerated in recent years as more and more persons discover the benefits of weight lifting. In this publication the authors offer a clear and sensible approach to weight training. These easy-to-follow techniques are geared towards the athlete, the fitness enthusiast, and the body builder. Its program can be followed by both men and women.

The authors begin with a presentation of the major theoretical concepts of weight training, then establish scientific precedence for training methods. Their explanation of the exercise is kinesiologically accurate and easily understood, augmented by ample illustrations. The authors' technique for measuring your own personal progress is invaluable, and their outline of weight control procedures and diets for competitors is excellent.

This work will serve as a boon to anyone with a desire for fitness and conditioning through weight training.

Murray Levin
National Chairman
AAU Weightlifting Committee

Until *Personalized Weight Training For Fitness and Athletics* was originally published in 1978, there was a paucity of text books available to students of weight training. This was particularly true at the college level, as I personally discovered while teaching weight training classes at the University of Washington and University of California, Berkeley. So, it's little wonder that *Personalized Weight Training for Fitness and Athletics* has been nationally and internationally adopted as a text by physical education teachers and coaches as well as health and fitness centers and corporations.

Above and beyond its application in the academic arena, this new edition of *Personalized Weight Training For Fitness and Athletics* will be useful to any of the nearly 20 million men and women currently involved in weight training across America, as well as to any athlete who wishes to improve his or her sports performance.

The clarity and depth of information in *Personalized Weight Training For Fitness and Athletics* is impressive, accurate, and expertly presented. The discussion of the scientific bases underlying practical weight training is particularly interesting, articulate, and valuable for all those involved at all levels of weight training.

I am sure that you will profit greatly from reading *Personalized Weight Training For Fitness and Athletics*.

Bill Reynolds
Editor-In-Chief
Muscle & Fitness Magazine

Preface

Upon reviewing the many texts and articles on the general subjects of weight training, weight lifting, strength fitness, conditioning or exercise programs, we have encountered one basic problem. While most texts offer a relatively complete overview of the field, none are arranged so that easy transfer from theoretical to practical aspects of training is accomplished. The student is not led in any clear, meaningful fashion from the physiological mechanisms underlying training technique to actual practice of them. All too frequently, random bits of physiological data are presented, usually serving to confuse the student further as to the "whys" and "hows" of training. Why does one train with weights in a particular way to maximize power, endurance, or size, for example?

This text was devised on the thesis that it is no longer appropriate or desirable simply to state that this is the way to do it. Students want to know why. By carefully selecting the most applicable physiological background information, this text elucidates the principles and techniques underlying the "whys" and "hows" of weight training.

Another focal point of the text is the fact that much misinformation, generally in the form of gym gossip, is spread concerning the so-called dangers, good points, methods and systems of weight training. This text, although far from complete, attempts to dispel many of these myths and misunderstandings by introducing the scientific approach to training technique and regimen selection. Along this line, sections on proper training regimens, nutrition, ergogenic aids, and beginners' through advanced students' regimen are provided. These sections are meant to serve as guidelines only, since every athlete or fitness enthusiast is confronted with problems which are largely personal. Therein lies the major contribution of the text—the personalized approach to training.

Another important contribution of the text is its applicability to women. Most texts on weight training either mention women's exercises in passing or fail to mention them at all. The approach used in this text is that women's training procedures and attendant physiological mechanisms are no different from those employed by men. The text is therefore applicable to both sexes.

Chapter 1 presents the physiological mechanisms which form the foundation of any weight training regimen. Chapter 2 addresses the basic principles of weight training as well as the myths associated with its practice, while Chapter 3 outlines the formulation of programmatic aims and objectives and offers suggestions concerning safety, injury, equipment and facility design. Chapter 4 deals with the various system approaches to the conduct of weight training and offers several examples of model weight training circuits. Chapter 5 describes and illustrates various specialized exercises, the appropriate apparatus involved, as well as offering a women's daily dozen training regimen. Chapter 6 discusses the nutritional dimensions of health and sport including implications concerning weight loss and ergogenic aids. Chapter 7 deals with charting training progress and assessment in an easily applied and unobtrusive sequence. A glossary of terms and units of measure associated with weight training is also presented as well as a selected bibliography and annotated periodical review that should serve as a key in opening the multidimensional domain of the art and science of weight training.

Traditionally covered topics such as training and rehabilitative exercise for the elderly and infirm, techniques of competitive weight lifting, calisthenics, and general training programs of a nonpersonalized nature have been purposely avoided.

The authors sincerely hope you have an enjoyable and informative experience when covering the text and incorporate weight training and vigorous physical activity as an integral dimension of your lifestyle.

Acknowledgments

The authors would like to express their sincere thanks to Clark Hatch Physical Fitness Centers and Fitness Systems, USA, Inc. for the use of their facilities in the preparation of the training photographs employed in the text. Deep gratitude is also extended to the late Floyd DeSpirito and A. Peter Thorne III who did much to shape the weight training career of the first author.

The authors also want to extend appreciation to Benjamin H. Massey, University of Illinois, Laurence E. Morehouse, University of California at Los Angeles, William Redden, University of Wisconsin, Robert Serfass and G. Alan Stull, University of Minnesota, and Wanda L. Thorpe, Professional Nutrition Services, Inc., Minneapolis, Minnesota for their helpful suggestions concerning the preparation of the manuscript. Deep gratitude is also extended to our wives, Joy and Leslie, and children Freddy, Disa Lee, Chip, and Rob, respectively, for their encouragement and love.

Frederick C. Hatfield
March L. Krotee

PERSONALIZED WEIGHT TRAINING FOR FITNESS AND ATHLETICS

From Theory to Practice

Muscle Physiology

Contents: *Gross Muscle Structure*
Muscle Fiber Structure
Other Structural Considerations
Blood Supply to Muscle Fibers
Nerve Supply to Muscle Fibers
Energetics of Anaerobic and Aerobic Pathways
Mechanics of Muscular Contraction
Types of Muscle Fiber

1

Introduction

There is a marked tendency for people to embrace simplistic approaches to problems. Taking the path of least resistance may often lead to equitable solutions and answers, but there are also instances that require relatively complex background information and understandings. Such is the case in weight training and conditioning. However, lest the reader immediately become turned off to the approach the present text espouses (there are many terms and phrases that are steeped in physiological jargon), it is the grasp of broad concepts that is important, not rote memorization of obscure facts. The reader is invited to become familiar with the general principles of weight training through an understanding of the mechanisms of his/her physiology. While it is desirable for one to remember selected facts, it is not necessary. Further, the end result one should strive for is proficiency in devising training regimen that conforms to basic principles of exercise science, a task which requires a personalized approach.

Gross Muscle Structure

Picture the last time you prepared a thick steak for dinner. The white lines running through the meat are comprised of connective tissue called *perimysium*. The perimysium binds bundles of *fibers* together into a *fasciculus*. Each fiber is actually a muscle cell which has its own connective tissue—the *endomysium*. Binding all the fasciculii together is yet another sheath of connective tissue called the *epimysium*. This is the outermost covering of the gross musculature.

Each muscle fiber—that is, each individual cell—transmits its contractile force to these various connective tissues. Since the connective tissues are continuous with the muscle's *tendons,* the force is thereby transmitted to the bones to which the tendons connect, resulting in movement.

A muscle fiber can range in size from about .01 millimeter to .10 millimeter in diameter, and from about 1.00 millimeter to many millimeters in length. The size of a fiber generally depends upon the location of the muscle—that is, the function of the muscle. Gross movements generally include muscles comprised of very long fibers, whereas fine movements such as ocular movements generally involve muscles with shorter fibers.

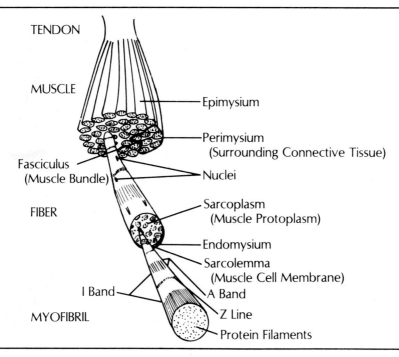

TENDON

MUSCLE

— Epimysium

— Perimysium
  (Surrounding Connective Tissue)

Fasciculus
(Muscle Bundle)

— Nuclei

FIBER

— Sarcoplasm
  (Muscle Protoplasm)

— Endomysium

— Sarcolemma
  (Muscle Cell Membrane)

I Band —

— A Band

MYOFIBRIL

— Z Line

— Protein Filaments

Figure 1.1. Construction of a section of skeletal muscle. An individual muscle fiber contains many myofibrils, and a fasciculus contains many muscle fibers. A muscle is a composite of many fasciculi. Adapted with permission of Macmillan Publishing Company from *The Human Body,* Second Edition by Sigmund Grollman. Copyright © 1969 by Sigmund Grollman.

Along the same line of reasoning, muscles are differentiated according to their arrangement of muscle fibers. There are two general classifications of skeletal muscles: *fusiform* and *penniform*. Fusiform muscles' fibers are arranged parallel to the long axis of the muscle, and are either long or short. *Long fusiform* muscles are relatively weak but contract a great distance. *Short fusiform* muscles are strong and have a very short contractile distance. Fusiform muscles are most commonly found in the extremities, although short fusiform muscles are found in the intercostal regions (i.e., between the ribs).

Penniform muscle fibers are arranged diagonally to the direction in which the muscle pulls. These muscles are found in the trunk as well as in the extremities. Because of the diagonal arrangement of the fibers, they do not contract over as great a distance as the fusiform muscles do, but are much stronger. There are three different classifications of penniform muscles: *unipennate,* with the fibers arranged on one side of the tendon; *bipennate,* with the fibers arranged on both sides of the tendon; and *multipennate,* with fibers attaching to several tendons.

Muscle Fiber Structure

The muscle cell—the contractile portion of the gross muscle—is surrounded by an extremely thin, semipermeable membrane called the *sarcolemma.* Just beneath the sarcolemma are the cell's *nucleii.* Within the fluid portion of the cell, the *sarcoplasm,* are the *myofibrils.*

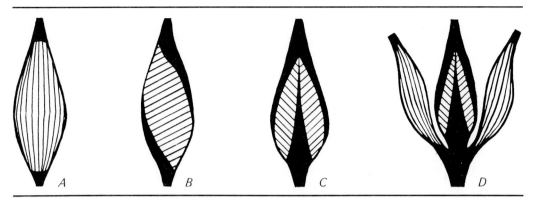

Figure 1.2. Diagrams showing kinds of arrangements of fibers of skeletal muscles. *A*, Fusiform. *B*, Unipennate. *C*, Bipennate. *D*, Multipennate. (Douglas.) From Rasch-Burke: *Kinesiology and Applied Anatomy* Sixth Edition, Lea & Febiger, Philadelphia, PA., 1978. Used by permission.

These myofibrils are the actual contractile units of each fiber, and are columnar structures of alternating light and dark segments. The coloring is due to the relative density of the overlapping protein filaments within each myofibril. Short, thick filaments of the protein *myosin* overlap with long, thin filaments of the protein *actin*. One "section" of these overlapping filaments is called a *sarcomere*.

Other Structural Considerations

There are other structures within each fiber that are related to its function. Tiny organelles, called *mitochondria,* are located between the myofibrils, and are responsible for the oxidative metabolism of the fibers as well as for the production ATP (adenosine triphosphate). More will be said on this subject later in the chapter. Other organelles of interest are the *sarcoplasmic reticulum* and transversely located tubules (called *t-tubules*). The t-tubules open to the exterior of the fiber and meet with the sarcoplasmic reticulum at strategic locations within the individual myofibrils. The sarcoplasmic reticulum is responsible for the storage and release of calcium ions, and, while the t-tubules are involved in this function also, they also are involved in the even distribution of the nerve impulse which triggers muscular contraction throughout the fiber.

Other subcellular structures are also important. *Ribosomes* are responsible for protein synthesis, especially during chronic exercise. *Myoglobin,* a red pigment, maintains the proper oxygen concentration within the fibers, allowing the mitochondria to function properly. *Glycogen granules* are located between the myofibrils for easy access, and are the "fuel" for energy production. Finally, various *enzymes* are present, and are collectively associated with the utilization of the glycogen (the storage form of carbohydrates found predominately in the muscles and liver).

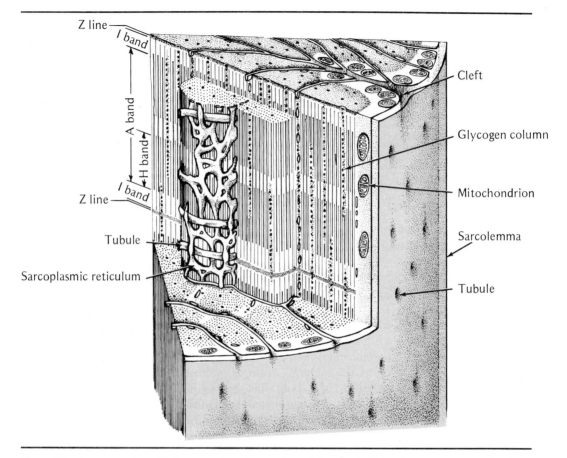

Figure 1.3. Structure of muscle fiber consists of a number of fibrils, which in turn are made up of orderly arrays of thick and thin filaments of protein. A system of transverse tubules opens to the exterior of the fiber. The sarcoplasmic reticulum is a system of tubules that does not open to the exterior. The two systems, which are evidently involved in the flow of calcium ions, meet at a number of junctions called dyads or triads. Mitochondria convert food to energy. The sarcolemma is a membrane surrounding the fiber. From *How Is Muscle Turned On and Off?* by Graham Hoyle. Copyright © 1970 by Scientific American, Inc. All rights reserved. Used by permission.

Blood Supply to Muscle Fibers

Arteries run from the heart through the spaces between the fasciculii, and branch into smaller *arterioles,* passing through the perimysium into the fasciculii. The arterioles then branch into tiny *capillaries* which service the individual muscle fibers. The exchange of foodstuffs and oxygen for metabolic waste material takes place at this level. The capillaries become *venioles,* and the venioles become *veins,* which return the waste-laden blood to the heart, and eventually to the lungs for elimination of the waste products. It seems somewhat unnecessary to state that the better the blood supply to the individual fibers, the more efficient will be the recovery rate of the exerciser. More will be said on this subject later.

Nerve Supply to Muscle Fibers

The functional unit involved in muscular innervation is the *motor unit*. Each motor unit has associated with it one *neuron* (nerve cell), with its *dendritic tree* and *axon*. The axon is a long, stringlike structure which carries the impulse to the fiber(s) of the motor unit. At the muscle, the axon branches into tiny *twigs,* which run to the individual fibers, and an *end plate* (also referred to as *terminal endings* or as the *myoneural junction*) attaches the twig with the sarcolemma of the muscle fibers (see Figure 1.4).

There may be from one to as many as one hundred separate muscle fibers innervated by a single neuron. Collectively, the neuron and all the muscle cells innervated by it are called a motor unit. An important point to remember is that the muscle fibers of any given motor unit are generally distributed throughout the gross muscle. That is, they are not all located close together. Another important point to remember is that when a motor unit is stimulated, all of the fibers associated with that motor unit contract fully. This is known as the "all-or-none" law of muscular contraction. However, since there are as many as fifty or more stimulations per second, or as few as ten or less, the amount of *tension* developed by the muscle allows for a finely *graded response*. This gradation of response in muscle tension is further facilitated by yet another mechanism called *asynchronous innervation.* Not all motor units are stimulated simultaneously, for if they were, fatigue would set in very rapidly, and all work would necessarily cease. Rather, when the *excitation threshold* of a motor unit is reached, it contracts and then relaxes while other motor units carry on the contraction. Perhaps an example of this mechanism will facilitate understanding. When you lift a fork to your mouth to eat, you initially perceive the weight of the fork to be minimal, and the stimulation is commensurately slight. However, when you perform the same curling movement with a dumbbell, the perception is different, and many more motor units are stimulated due to the greater amount of millivoltage reaching the muscle involved. If the dumbbell were a fake, an embarrassingly large number of motor units would have been stimulated and the weight would literally fly off the floor. This built-in gradation mechanism, then, allows for both extremely fine movements to occur as well as for allowing muscle fibers a chance to recuperate while others take over.

Generally, the muscles involved in fine movements are comprised of motor units with relatively few muscle fibers, whereas muscles involved in gross movements are comprised of motor units with a great number of muscle fibers. As mentioned earlier, the impulse from the end plate travels down the sarcolemma and throughout the network of t-tubules, allowing for simultaneous stimulation of all the muscle fiber's myofibrils.

Located between the muscle fibers is an important *proprioceptor* known as the *muscle spindle*. The significance of the muscle spindle is its ability to detect, respond to and control alterations in the length of the muscle fiber. Actually a modified muscle fiber, this mechanism is stimulated when the surrounding muscle fibers are stretched, and the resultant stimulation is sent back to the *alpha motor neurons* which innervate the same muscle fibers. The appropriate motor units are thereby stimulated, and the muscle contracts in opposition to the original stretch placed on the muscle. This is known as the *stretch reflex,* and has as its most common example the knee-jerk reflex. There are many instances in sport and weight lifting wherein this mechanism may be used to the athlete's advantage. Another point involving this stretch reflex must be discussed before leaving the subject, however. At the same time the stretched muscles are called upon to react to the stretch they have been placed under; other "helping" muscles

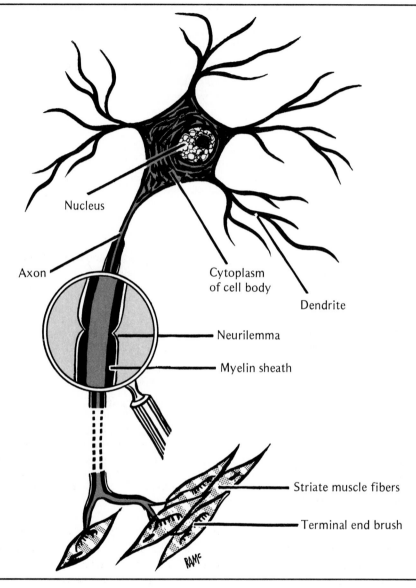

Figure 1.4. A diagrammatic drawing of a neuron. At the top is the cell body and its numerous branchings, the dendrites. They make up the soma of the neuron. The axon, of which there is only one, extends downward. The point at which the axon leaves the soma is the axon hillock. Axons, and sometimes dendrites, may be covered with a myelin sheath, and, outside the nervous system, with a neurilemma. From Morgan and Stellar, *Physiological Psychology.* Copyright © 1950 by McGraw-Hill Book Company. Used by permission.

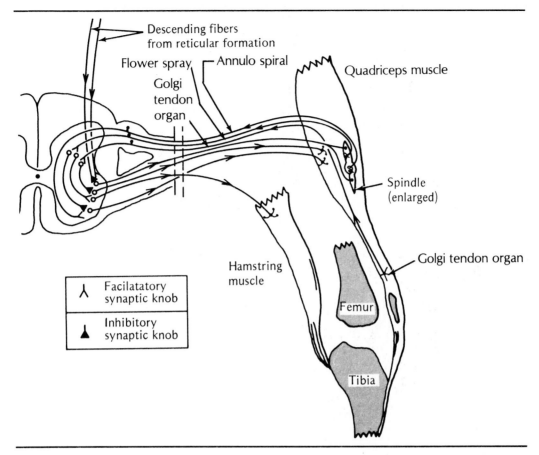

Figure 1.5. The myotatic and inverse myotatic reflexes as "autogenetic governors" of movement at the knee joint. Note that supraspinal influence, both facilitatory and inhibitory is brought to bear on the gamma efferent neuron thus setting the bias of the spindle. From deVries: *Physiology of Exercise* Third Edition. Wm. C. Brown Company Publishers, 1983. Used by permission.

called *synergists* and *stabilizer* muscles are brought into play also. Their contraction aids the stretched muscles to respond. Also, there is a general inhibition of the stretched muscle's *antagonists*. These are the muscles which are in opposition to the contracting muscle (called the *protagonist* when spoken of in conjunction with the antagonist). For example, when the stretch reflex causes the biceps to contract, the muscles located on the back of the arm, the triceps, are simultaneously inhibited from contracting, allowing for facilitated contracture of the bicep. This chain of events is called *reciprocal innervation*. The stretch reflex also serves as a self regulating or compensating mechanism that enables the muscle to adjust automatically (reflex arc) to differences in load and length without immediate feedback from higher order centers (cerebellum).

Working with the muscle spindles is yet another proprioceptor called the *golgi tendon organ.* This mechanism, located in the tendon of the muscle, is stimulated when stretched by a connected contracting muscle. Its functions are twofold: first, they relay information about the force of contracture to the central nervous system, allowing for just the right amount of force to be applied while lifting an object; secondly, they serve to protect the muscle from damage from excessive tension. This second function is accomplished by inhibiting further contraction of the protagonist, and stimulating a corresponding contracture of the antagonist. In this fashion the golgi tendon's prime function may be thought to be protective in nature to the muscle and its connective tissue especially when attempting to lift excessive loads.

Energetics of Anaerobic and Aerobic Pathways

Energy (primarily from food ingestion) for muscular contraction is stored within the muscle in the form of two high energy compounds. One such compound involved in muscular contraction is that of adenosine triphosphate (ATP) which has been previously mentioned. As muscular contraction continues, the stores of this organic compound are broken down to produce inorganic compounds and energy (ATP $\rightarrow$ ADP + P + E). This is the energy used for contraction. However, these ATP stores are quickly depleted, and another organic compound called *phosphocreatine* (PC) is broken down so that the energy released in its breakdown can combine with the ADP to resynthesize ATP for additional energy for contraction. This reaction is summarized as follows: PC $\rightarrow$ C + P + E. Again, however, this process cannot continue, because the PC is also quickly depleted. At this point, glycogen is broken down to yield the energy required to replenish the stores of phosphocreatine so that it can in turn be broken down to resynthesize ATP. As the glycogen is broken down, lactic acid and energy are released. It would now appear that the process is complete; that is, the organic phosphates are continuously resynthesized. The stores of glycogen are also being depleted, however, and lactic acid, a waste product which retards contraction, is accumulating as a result of the glycogen breakdown. The equilibrium of this process, therefore, is not maintained; if it were, muscular contraction could last only about 30 seconds due to the buildup of lactic acid and the depletion of glycogen. Thus far in the process, no oxygen has been used to produce contraction. Therefore, the process to this point is referred to as the *anaerobic* pathway.

Oxygen being introduced into the process allows two more chemical reactions to occur. Oxygen combines with about one-fifth of the built-up lactic acid to produce energy. This energy is used to convert the remaining four-fifths of the lactic acid back into glycogen. The water and carbon dioxide produced in the first reaction are passed off via the circulatory system and expelled by the lungs during normal breathing. The entire chain is summarized in Figure 1.6. It should be clearly understood, however, that both the processes summarized here and in Figure 1.6 are just that—summaries. For a complete description and sequence of the complex biochemical processes involved in the synthesis and breakdown of the energy sources of muscular contraction, the reader is directed to some of the exercise physiology books mentioned in the bibliography section of this text. The portion of the reactions summarized which involve the utilization of oxygen is called the aerobic pathway. Work can now continue indefinitely, provided that sufficient oxygen is present to interact with the lactic acid.

1. Organic Phosphate → Inorganic Phosphate + Organic Phosphate + Energy
   ATP   →   P   +   ADP   + Energy
   (Adenosine tri-   (Phosphate)   (Adenosine di-
   Phosphate)   Phosphate)

2. Organic Phosphate + Organic Phosphate → Organic Phosphate + Organic Mineral
   PC   +   ADP   →   ATP   +   C
   (Phospho-   (Adenosine di-   (Adenosine tri-   (Creatine)
   creatine)   Phosphate)   Phosphate)

3. Glycogen → Lactic Acid + Energy for resynthesis of PC
   (i.e., for putting 'P' from 1 and 'C' from 2 back together)

4. Organic Mineral + Inorganic Phosphate + Energy → Organic Phosphate
   C   +   P   + Energy →   PC

5. 1/5 Lactic Acid + O_2 → CO_2 + H_2O + Energy for resynthesis of remainder
   Lactic Acid

6. 4/5 Lactic Acid + Energy (from 5) + O_2 → Glycogen

Figure 1.6. Summary of anaerobic and aerobic pathways.

As work becomes progressively intense, and the circulatory system becomes incapable of supplying sufficient oxygen to oxidize the lactic acid, fatigue sets in. A buildup of less than a few tenths of 1% of the lactic acid concentration in a muscle results in muscular pain and a cessation of contraction. This type of fatigue is the most common and is normally accompanied by an *oxygen debt*. Expressing it another way, the amount of oxygen it would take to oxidize the built-up lactic acid is "owed" to the system, and one's "tolerance" for an accumulated debt is generally proportional to his or her aerobic fitness.

As can be seen from the above path analyses, the anaerobic pathway provides for heavy but short duration bouts of exercise and is quite inefficient in the generation of ATP (approximately 1:36 molecules of ATP) when compared to the aerobic pathway. Another illustration of the two pathways is presented in Figure 1.7.

Mechanics of Muscular Contraction

In the previously discussed section on muscle cell structure, it was mentioned that muscle fibers consisted of the sarcolemma, nucleii, sarcoplasm, and myofibrils, together with other smaller organelles and subcellular structures. This section deals with the mechanics of myofibrillar contraction.

An electrical impulse arriving at the motor end plate of the fibers causes the release of *acetylcholine* (ACh), a chemical which initiates a disturbance of the permeability of the sarcolemma. This disturbance travels down the sarcolemma and through the t-tubules to release calcium from the sarcoplasmic reticula. Prolonged stimulation causes the vesicles which release the ACh to diminish. However, generally before this can occur, another chemical, *acetylcholinesterase,* destroys the ACh and returns the sarcolemma to its former stability. It is the release of calcium which triggers contraction.

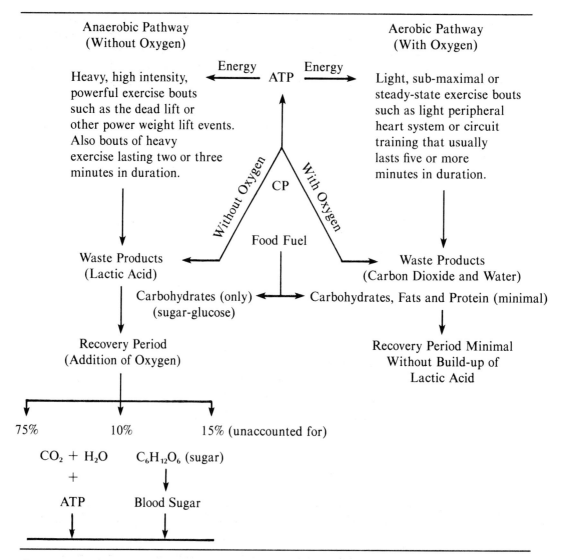

Figure 1.7. The anaerobic and aerobic pathways for the resynthesizing of energy (ATP) to sustain physical activity.

The released calcium binds with a regulatory protein called *troponin,* which is located on the long, thin actin filaments within the myofibrils. This bond causes an interaction between the actin and myosin filaments such that they are forced through a change in conformation. This conformational change involves the production of a "pulling force" between the actin and myosin filaments. The process is reversed upon the destruction of ACh (i.e., upon relaxation).

Prevalent theory in exercise physiology has it that the mechanism involved in the sliding of the actin and myosin filaments across each other to produce muscular contraction is actually similar to tiny "cross–bridges" grabbing, releasing, and regrabbing their way across each other (see Figure 1.8). Since the actin filaments are connected to the portion of the sarcomere referred to as the Z-line, this pulling action draws the two ends of the sarcomere together. As this process continues, the force exerted by the sliding filaments is transmitted to the connective tissues of the muscle, then to the tendons which act on the bones to which they are attached. Further structural changes associated with myofibrillar contraction may be found in Figure 1.9.

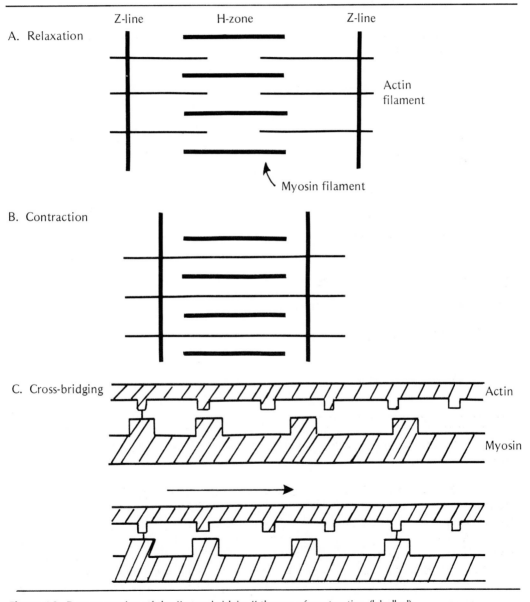

Figure 1.8. Representation of the "cross-bridging" theory of contraction (labelled).

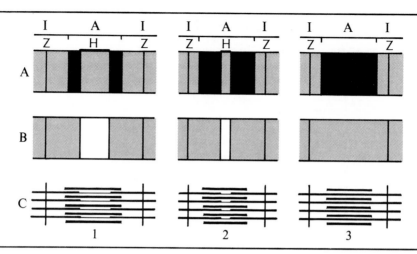

Figure 1.9. Diagram illustrating the structural changes associated with contraction *(3)* and extension *(1)* from resting length *(2)*. **A** shows the band patterns of intact fibril. **B** shows the band patterns after extraction of myosin. **C** shows the positions of the filaments. (From Huxley, H. E., and Hanson, J., in *The Structure and Function of Muscle.* G. H. Bourne, ed., 1960. Courtesy of the Academic Press, New York.

Types of muscular contraction. While the mechanics of muscular contraction are basically the same for all types of contractions, it is necessary to describe their differences. These differences will be vital to a basic understanding of various systems of training to be discussed in a later chapter.

Isometric contraction of a muscle occurs when the weight being lifted is too heavy to move (e.g., pushing against a brick wall or pulling at a weight which is too heavy to budge). In this instance, cross–bridging occurs, but not to the extent that movement is caused, or, rather, not to the extent that a shortening of the muscle occurs.

Isotonic contraction, on the other hand, does involve an actual shortening of the muscle. This process is clearly illustrated during the "curling" of a weight held in the hand. You will notice the biceps bulge at the middle while the weight is being lifted. This bulge is the result of the sarcomeres being drawn toward one another during the cross–bridging process. The shortening of the muscle during isotonic contraction is referred to as *concentric* contraction, because of the acted-upon limb's movement toward the contracting muscle. When the same weight used in the example above is lowered, another form of isotonic contraction is involved— *eccentric* contraction. In eccentric contraction, the cross–bridges apparently are raked across each other in an effort to shorten, but the intensity, or frequency, of innervation is not great enough to allow this to happen. This "raking" is similar to pulling two toothbrushes across one another, and it results in a high amount of friction. This concept will be referred to again later in the text. It has been found that concentric contraction of a muscle involves considerably more motor units than does eccentric contraction, a fact which explains the relatively greater energy expenditure during concentric work. However, this phenomenon applies only if the same amount of weight are involved in both forms of contraction. Far greater amounts of weight can

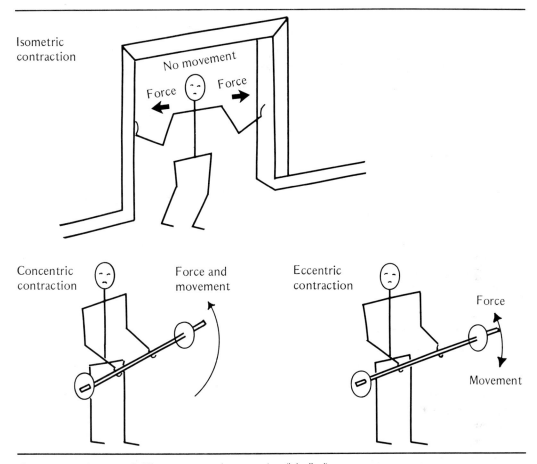

Figure 1.10. Diagram of different types of contraction (labelled).

be lowered in an eccentric movement, for example, than can be lifted during a concentric movement. This has prompted some weight trainers to use a system of training involving the use of eccentric contracture. The term used to describe this method of training has been *negative resistance* training, to which further reference will be made later in the text.

The term and training procedure that has recently attempted to employ the advantages and eliminate the disadvantages of isometric and isotonic contraction is that of *isokinetics*. In isokinetic training the resistance adjusts concomitantly with the maximum force throughout the entire range of the lift. Research to date has yet to compare the traditional zero velocity (isometric), the standard 5-RM to 10-RM (isotonic) training or combination thereof such as "functional isometric" training where 1-RM (Maximal Repetition) is held against a fixed position (i.e., power rack) for a short time duration.

Types of Muscle Fiber

The last time you dined on chicken, did you prefer the dark meat or did you dig in to the white portion? Have you ever wondered why such differentiation of muscle tissue occurs? Chickens are ground birds, so their wing muscles (the breast) are adapted to short, powerful flights only, and their legs are correspondingly adapted to bearing their weight. The same type of differentiation of muscle tissue is present in humans although species-related considerations must be accounted for. Within the human skeletal muscles there seem to be distinct fiber types which have been identified by their contractile (twitch contraction time) and other various metabolic characteristics. Although many classifications of muscle fiber typing are evident in the current research literature i.e., Type II A,B,etc., only the primary fiber types will be addressed by the authors.

Red muscle fiber, or *slow-twitch* fiber (Type I), has greater oxidative capacity than does white muscle fiber, or *fast-twitch* (Type II). That is, slow-twitch fibers have a greater endurance (aerobic) capacity. The endurance of a muscle is closely related to the size and number of mitochondria, the extent of capillarization around the fibers, the concentration of glycogen stores, and the concentration of myoglobin. The myoglobin is responsible for the red coloration of slow-twitch muscle fibers. These factors enable the muscle to produce energy for contraction over a long period of time since anaerobic and aerobic pathways are considerably enhanced by the presence of these factors.

The speed and tension of muscular contraction, however, are dependent on properties which differ from those involved in muscular endurance. The speed at which a muscle contracts is closely related to the rate at which ATP can be utilized; and this ability is related to the presence of related enzymes and the extensiveness of the sarcoplasmic reticulum network. The amount of tension produced by a muscle (that is, the strength of the muscle's contraction) is also closely related to enzyme activity, but other less apparent factors are more important. The amount of myofibrillar protein per cross-sectional area is important, for example. So, too, is the number of muscle fibers in the muscle as well as the number of fibers in each motor unit.

Thus, a three-way classification system has emerged, involving the speed, tension, and endurance of muscle fibers. With regard to speed, white muscle fibers appear to be best suited, but they vary considerably, however, in their endurance capacity. A muscle fiber may be fast-twitch and have high- or low-oxidative capacity, or it may be slow-twitch. Generally, slow-twitch fibers vary less than fast-twitch in their oxidative capacity—all are generally fatigue resistant. The tension capacity of a muscle is closely related to the speed of contraction. Thus, fast-twitch fibers are generally also the strongest.

Another point should be made regarding the speed capacity of slow- and fast-twitch fibers. There is some speculation that the relatively thicker nerves servicing the fast-twitch fibers are responsible for their greater shortening speed. This point tends to corroborate what experience has shown the majority of weight trainers—that selection of specific types of exercises performed at specific speeds, intensities, and durations have selective effects on the different muscle fiber types. One can train specifically for endurance, speed, and/or strength. More will be said on this principle of specificity later.

While certain types of exercise can cause changes in concentrations of various factors within a muscle fiber (e.g., fast-twitch fibers that had a low-oxidative capacity can become fast-twitch with a higher oxidative capacity), the ratio of fast-twitch and slow-twitch fibers is genetically determined and cannot be changed through training. Muscle biopsies performed on champion sprinters and long-distance swimmers confirm the fact that this inherited ratio predetermines an athlete's capacity to achieve in these activities. The sprinter was born with a preponderance of fast-twitch fibers, while the long-distance swimmer inherited a preponderance of the red, slow-twitch fibers that are suited to endurance activity. Many countries are now engaged in preselection of athletes for certain sports, basically through reference to these considerations. While such preselection techniques have obvious advantages, it seems that in our society, with strong pressures to preserve such basic human rights as freedom of choice, such practices seem to be futuristic in nature. However, these authors anticipate more research employing the biopsy technique in the very near "Olympic" future.

Figure 1.11 provides the reader with a view of the muscle fiber composition of athletes representing various sports including weight lifting.

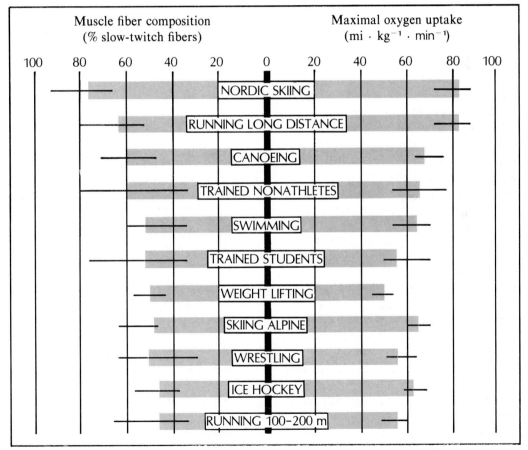

Figure 1.11. Muscle fiber composition (percent slow-twitch fibers) (left side) and maximal oxygen uptake (right side) in athletes representing different sports. The dark horizontal bar denotes the range. (From Bergh, U. et al.: Maximal oxygen uptake and muscle fiber types in trained and untrained humans. Med. Sci. Sports *10*:151, 1978. Copyright 1978, the American College of Sports Medicine. Reprinted by permission.)

Basic Principles of Training

Contents: *Basic Principles of Weight Training*

2

Chapter 1 dealt with the structural and functional mechanisms of muscular contraction. The basic principles described therein are the basis for selecting and performing exercise regimen. One cannot expect to increase a muscle's power, for example, by performing exercises which solely isolate red or slow-twitch fibers. White or fast-twitch fibers are also most important in power or anaerobic movements, while red fibers are called upon primarily in endurance or aerobic efforts. Thus, a basic group of principles emerges which will aid the exerciser in achieving personal fitness objectives in an efficient and maximized manner.

Basic Principles of Weight Training

Probably the most basic principle of exercise is that the body grows and develops in efficiency and size with exercise and deteriorates with disuse. This is referred to as the *law of use and disuse.* This law can be clearly seen by observing the circumference of a limb before and after it has been placed in a cast for several weeks. The limb's musculature undergoes severe *atrophy,* and the joints become relatively immobile. Mobility is returned only after weeks of use, and the muscles also return to their previous size after a similar period of time and use. Muscles seem to adapt to the demands placed upon them in highly specific ways. That is through increasing the amount of stress (work) on a muscle, the muscles enhance their ability to develop higher levels of tension (strength) and to perform more work over time (endurance). Although significant strength gains seem to be developed most efficiently through working with high-resistance, low repetition-training or specific training; this phenomenon is referred to as the SAID principle (Specific Adaptation to Imposed Demands); some less significant and specific gains in endurance may also be realized.

Adaptation generally involves another dimension also—that of overcompensation. Callus develops in the hands as an adaptation to friction, muscle fibrils which are splintered in animals (not substantiated in humans) during heavy exercise often grow in both size and number, lacerated tissue develops new "scar" tissue in greater amounts than the original tissue, and proliferation of connective tissue and satellite cells surrounding the muscle fiber thickens and strengthens the muscle's connective tissue harness. These are examples of a specific class of adaptation responses referred to as the *law of overcompensation.*

Related to these basic principles is the notion that adaptation and overcompensation can occur only if the particular structure is taxed beyond that level which it normally is accustomed. Adaptation must be induced. By progressively increasing the stress placed on the muscles, one forces the muscles to adapt. This is referred to as the *overload principle.*

Since many human forms of movement require the use of many different muscles, it seems that only the weaker muscles involved in the movement are being taxed maximally, the stronger ones bearing the stresses of the movement with ease. These larger or stronger muscles will not adapt to great stress unless great stress is placed upon them. Consequently, there must be some means of isolating them so as to alleviate the problem of smaller, weaker muscles limiting the amount of stress that can be placed on them. In weight training, this need is accounted for by the array of exercises and specialized apparatuses used. The *isolation principle* is the key to selecting the appropriate exercise, while the SAID and *overload* principles are the keys to how that exercise should be performed.

With the preceding principles in mind, we can now progress to a discussion of the specific factors involved in training, and basic methods of achieving desired outcomes.

Factors Involved in Muscular Strength

Generally, the strength of contraction of a single muscle fiber is related to the ability of the contractile elements to contract, producing tension. As was discussed earlier, white, fast-twitch muscle fibers are generally more capable of producing higher tension than are red, slow-twitch fibers, presumably due to more efficient enzyme activity and nerve fiber properties. It is not clear as to whether there is a direct causal relationship between strength and fiber hypertrophy; nor is it clear whether hypertrophy of individual fibers is due to increased size and numbers of myofibrils or to an increase in the amount of sarcoplasm, or both. It is, however, a purely theoretical concept at this level. What is really important is the strength of the entire muscle and the amount of force that can be produced at the ends of the bony levers.

Gross muscular strength is related to (1) the arrangement of muscle fibers (i.e., fusiform or penniform), (2) the number of motor units being stimulated simultaneously, (3) the preponderance of white versus red fibers, and (4) an innominate factor, involving what may be considered social and psychological motivation affecting the ability of the exerciser to concentrate on the specific muscle being contracted. In any event, the fourth factor probably can be reduced to the fact that more motor units are recruited in the effort.

The amount of force that can be produced at the ends of the bony levers, however, involves additional factors. Coordinating the actions of all the muscles involved in the movement, for example, will result in greater force application. This coordinated effort involves the *prime movers,* the helping *synergists,* and the *stabilizers.* Prime movers are those muscles whose fibers are arranged such that their contraction most aids the movement, and synergistic muscles are those whose fibers help, but only minimally, due to their nonadvantageous angle of attachment. Stabilizer muscles contract isometrically to render other body parts immovable during the desired movement, and are generally located nearer the origin of the prime movers.

The efficiency of the lever system involved is of paramount importance. An example of such leverage is illustrated in Figure 2.1. Notice that if the force arm (distance between muscle's insertion and the axis) is lengthened, the resultant force will be greater. This general principle applies to most of the lever systems in the body, as only a few of them are other than third-class levers. Needless to say, the length of any given force arm is an inherited trait. One can readily see the advantage an athlete with good leverage would have over one who didn't. Far more muscular force would be needed by athletes lacking efficient leverage in order to lift the same amount of weight.

With the preceding knowledge regarding the source(s) of muscular strength, it should become quite clear that, in most activities, strength alone is of little value. Explosive strength, on the other hand, is essential. *Power* is the rate of doing work, while strength is merely the amount of force which a muscle is able to produce. Thus, power can be thought of as being resultant of two factors, speed, which increases the rate at which force can be applied, and strength, which produces the force. One has, therefore, three methods at his or her disposal by which to increase power: (1) increase your strength, (2) increase your speed, or (3) increase both. While speed can be improved, the amount of improvement will be minimal. Generally, speed increments are a result of learning to coordinate efforts of muscles involved, and learning to achieve

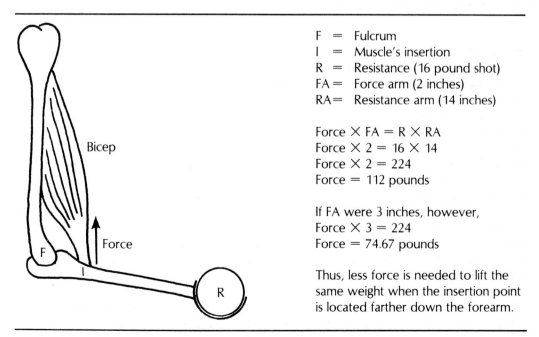

F = Fulcrum
I   = Muscle's insertion
R = Resistance (16 pound shot)
FA = Force arm (2 inches)
RA= Resistance arm (14 inches)

Force × FA = R × RA
Force × 2 = 16 × 14
Force × 2 = 224
Force = 112 pounds

If FA were 3 inches, however,
Force × 3 = 224
Force = 74.67 pounds

Thus, less force is needed to lift the same weight when the insertion point is located farther down the forearm.

Bicep

Force

F

I

R

Figure 2.1. The arm acting as a third class lever. The formula for determining the amount of force applied.

maximal recruitment of appropriate fibers. Thus, since such learning normally occurs rapidly, noticeable gains in speed are made, after which gains become minimal. Strength, on the other hand, can be increased markedly and over a long period of time. The authors' research and experience concerning weight training classes within a ten week, two to three times per week exercise regimen reveal that strength gains by both men and women range between 15%–28%. Most high school and college athletes have not even begun to reach their full strength potential.

Methods of Strength Development

The amount of *tension* produced by a muscle is the key to significant strength increases. Although some research has indicated that strength gains may occur during sub-maximal training, it is recommended that for maximal gains in explosive strength to occur, loads greater than two-thirds of one's maximum limit be employed, and preferably 80%–90% of one's maximal lifting (1-RM) capacity. Since the fuel for such activity is the organic phosphates ATP and PC, which are depleted very rapidly during explosive movements, the *duration* and *frequency* of the exercise must be such that these energy substrate are resynthesized. Should contractions continue beyond about ten seconds, aerobic mechanisms begin to mobilize and the amount of tension developed by the muscle generally falls below the critical two-thirds limit. Consequently, four to six repetitions (completed in less than ten seconds) are recommended. There should be a brief rest between sets to allow resynthesis of ATP and PC to occur. About three to six sets of four to six repetitions should be performed, again with near-maximum weight. Each repetition should be performed explosively, to accommodate the learning factor.

Upon repeated depletion of energy substrate, overcompensation takes place. That is, stores of ATP and PC become more abundant. This allows one to continue contraction for a longer period, perhaps, but is not related to increased muscular strength. This is what is called *strength endurance,* not to be confused with muscular or cardiovascular endurance. Again, strength increases are due to the learning factor and to the increased efficiency, or the *quality,* of the myofibrillar elements in producing tension.

It should be pointed out that strength training is highly specific. Only the motor units involved will benefit from exercise, and it is maximum effort per repetition which stimulates other, previously unused, motor units. Furthermore, such training will not improve the tension capacity of other muscles—only those involved in the overload process will benefit significantly. During isotonic contractions of the type mentioned above, only a very small portion of the total movement will be overloaded if the degree of effort remains constant over the entire movement. This is true because the angle of the muscle's insertion into the bony lever determines how much weight can be lifted. For example, the elbow joint and flexor muscle may be stronger between 100°–140° than it is below or above that angle of flexion. Consequently, the muscle is being overloaded only during the portion of the movement wherein the muscle is weakest. To circumvent this problem, one must attempt to maximally contract the biceps throughout the full range of movement, and must, correspondingly, accelerate the movement to such a degree that the ballistic, or momentum, factor is minimized. What the exerciser must strive to do, therefore, is to recruit as large a number of motor units as possible at every angle throughout the movement, thus allowing for efficient overload at every angle. This practice is referred to as *compensatory acceleration,* and may be dangerous if not performed properly, owing to the momentum

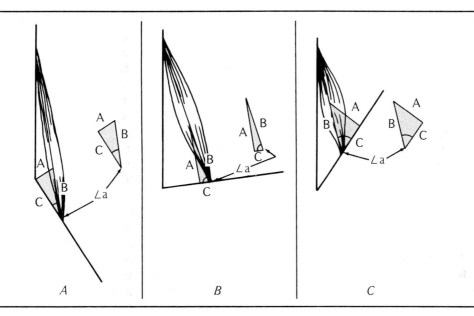

Figure 2.2. Effect of the angle of pull of a muscle upon the external force (A) provided for equal amounts of internal muscular force (B). Side (C) in each case represents wasted internal force. From deVries: *Physiology of Exercise* Third Edition. Wm. C. Brown Publishers, 1983. Used by permission.

imparted to weights during the accelerative movement having to be reversed just prior to reaching the end of the movement. If the acceleration is not reversed, the joint involved will bear the brunt of the stress. However, with practice, compensatory acceleration can overcome the disadvantages of differential leverage factors limiting overload to only a small portion of a given movement.

Factors Involved in Muscular Hypertrophy

The most noticeable effect of weight training is that muscles grow larger over a period of time. This effect is called *hypertrophy,* and is generally due to the overcompensation principle. Again, as in strength development, muscles grow by applying overload, and only those fibers directly stimulated will significantly hypertrophy. It is probable that all elements of the muscle are increased through hypertrophy training. The myofibrils increase in size and number, the connective tissues become thicker, sarcoplasmic content is increased, and increased numbers of capillaries are caused to appear. Thus, for maximal hypertrophy, variation in exercise methods is important, since many of the muscle's elements are increased in size, number, quantity and/ or function differentially.

Myofibrillar hypertrophy may be included through actions related to nervous system functioning. As mentioned earlier (Chapter 1), the nerves which service white, fast-twitch fibers are thicker than those which service the red, slow-twitch fibers. This anatomical difference, it is believed, accounts for the fast versus slow-twitch fibers. This anatomical difference, it is believed, accounts for the fast- versus slow-twitch properties of the respective fibers. This fact also tends to explain why white fiber myofibrils have the capacity for greater hypertrophy than do the red fibers myofibrils.

On the other hand, red fibers, rich in myoglobin, mitochondria, and capillaries, are more suited to aerobic work than are the white fibers. There are some white fibers, however, which possess high-oxidative capacity similar to the red fibers. While they are fast-twitch, they also are fatigue-resistant. By taxing their fatigue resistance via overload endurance training, these fibers respond by becoming more resistant to fatigue through developing greater amounts of myoglobin and capillaries.

Since the tension produced by the myofibrils causes a pull at all of the surrounding connective tissues and the muscle's tendons, a thickening of the connective tissue and tendons occurs so as to compensate for the increased tension placed on them. Again we see the principle of overcompensation operating. Generally, forceful, fast contractions will cause this thickening as well as the increased hypertrophy of the myofibrillar elements, while slow, submaximal, continuous contractions will cause increases in oxygen demands of the red fibers, thereby causing increases in capillaries, myoglobin, mitochondria, and enzyme concentrations.

Methods of Hypertrophy Development

As pointed out earlier, variation of method is a key concept in training for hypertrophy. The greatest amount of muscular hypertrophy stems from the overcompensation effect of increased size and number of myofibrillar elements within the muscle fiber. High-speed work with a load of 60% of one's maximum for about fifteen repetitions and four–six sets will yield this effect, but the strength and muscular endurance benefits will not be as significant employing this level of regimen. For strength to increase along with increases in hypertrophy, loads of 80% or greater must be used. This system involves doing high-speed movements for about six–eight repetitions for a similar number of sets. Again, recall that tension is the key to strength development; it is assumed that far more weight can be handled if the number of repetitions performed is low. At the other end of the spectrum, performing an exercise for thirty or more repetitions with extremely light weights (less than 40%), and maintaining a slow, continuous cadence, is more suited to developing the red fibers' elements—the mitochondria, capillaries, myoglobin, and enzymes. Additionally, though more research is needed in this area, this type of training may tend to convert some of the white, fast-twitch fibers to the point where their oxidative capacity is increased. Far less hypertrophy occurs in such a system than those involving strictly fast-twitch fibers. Again the SAID principle should be applied.

Many lifters interested in hypertrophy (or body-building, as it is commonly called) rely on a system of training called *forced repetition* training. Here, the lifter performs the exercise to fatigue, and then, by sheer willpower or concentration, forces the muscles to respond by performing two or more additional repetitions. Such a system seems at odds with the principle of avoiding fatigue (mentioned under strength development), since the critical percentage of maximum would not be achieved. However, the theory is that by forcing out additional repetitions, one calls upon as yet unused motor units to respond, thereby lowering their threshold of excitation so that they can be called upon with greater ease later. As this process continues, recruitment of such unused fibers becomes more and more difficult. The cliché that one must "train through pain in order to gain" is a widespread belief in the world of body-building, and such a system has produced the greatest physique artists in history. Notwithstanding this notion's popularity, however, for *complete* development to occur, variations in the forced repetitions system of the type already mentioned are recommended. In other words, forced repetitions can be done while performing the 40%, 60%, or 80% systems—there need not be any disagreement on this point.

Inasmuch as hypertrophy training requires a rather diversified program, involving elements from both strength and endurance training as well as some elements unique to itself, it is the system most recommended for the general fitness enthusiast. Women concerned about substantial muscle size and girth gains need not be overly worried as due to a lack of the male hormone testosterone (tissue builder) the female capability to significantly hypertrophy seems limited. Moderate gains in both strength and muscular and strength endurance components can be realized along with a more appealing physique. Body-building, as an art and sport, has far surpassed weight lifting in popularity in this country, and the various benefits which can be derived are probably at the root of this popularity. For overall fitness, however, one must consider the cardiovascular and cardiorespiratory systems as well. More will be said on the matter of overall physical fitness later in the text.

Factors Involved in Muscular Endurance

The adaptive changes which take place as a result of endurance training overlap only minimally with those occurring during strength and hypertrophy training. Very little size and strength increase takes place in such training, as the adaptations occur largely under the umbrella of the aerobic pathway. It is entirely possible for muscular endurance to increase substantially as a result of strength and hypertrophy training, but far more efficient and complete muscular endurance development can be obtained through calling upon the aerobic pathway. That is, by overloading the muscles so that their need for oxygen is increased, adaptation of the mechanisms involved in the oxidative process are increased in size, numbers, and/or function.

Repeated, submaximal contractions cause a reddening of some of the white fibers as a result of increased myoglobin concentrations which also cause the red fibers to become redder. Recall that the myoglobin's function was to maintain a proper oxygen concentration in the fibers. However, for this to be possible, there must be more oxygen. Adaptive increases occur, therefore, in the size and numbers of mitochondria, which are responsible for the oxidative metabolism of the muscle as well as the synthesis of ATP. Also, an adaptive buildup of capillaries surrounding the fiber occurs. New capillaries are thought to be formed as a result of the continued contraction; it is also possible that other, previously dormant, capillaries are opened through the same process. The muscle's glycogen stores are also elevated. Additionally, changes occur within the nervous system which are designed to allow greater repetition of, or greater length of, muscular contraction. In any case, noted gains in strength or size as a result of endurance training are relatively minimal (probably as a result of reversing some of the effects of disuse). They do not continue to increase to any significant extent beyond the first two or three weeks of training.

Courtesy of James L. Shaffer

Courtesy of University of Wisconsin

Courtesy of Southern Connecticut State College

Courtesy of Strix Pix

Courtesy of Lynn D. Howell

Figure 2.3. The various sporting endeavors depicted here require different physical attributes. The wise coach or athlete should identify the components of fitness most essential in his/her sport, and select the most appropriate avenue to acquire them. One of the important points of this text is to elucidate the importance of adhering to the basic principles of conditioning, whatever the desired outcome or avenue chosen to achieve it.

A. These swimmers are competing in the butterfly event. The short distance covered in this event necessitates concentrating on both power as well as local muscular endurance while other events covering greater distances would require primarily cardiovascular endurance.

B. This high jumper must possess exceptional leg power to propel his body upwards. Other muscles, acting as synergists (or, helpers) must be powerful also, including lower back and arm elevator muscles. The so-called ``Fosbury Flop'' technique requires exceptional coordination as well.

C. Aside from the high degree of coordination required to put the shot, this female athlete must possess explosive power in all body segments, in order that the sum of all muscular forces generated while crossing the circle are transferred maximally to the shot. Weight training techniques for women are identical to those engaged in by male athletes. The outburst of record-breaking performances in recent years by female athletes can be traced to the acceptance of weight training as an essential part of their training regimen.

D. This Olympic-style weightlifter has just consumated a successful 300-pound press (a lift no longer contested in international competition). Olympic weightlifters must possess exceptional explosive power, strength and strength endurance. Note the extent of muscular hypertrophy in comparison to that of the shot putter or distance runner.

E. Cross-country running requires cardiovascular and cardiorespiratory endurance. The slim physique of the runner bespeaks the importance of red (slow-twitch) muscle fiber, while the weightlifter depicted requires primarily white (fast-twitch) muscle fiber.

F. Crew members (coxswain excluded) are generally taller than average, and possess great local muscular endurance in the legs, lower back, shoulders and biceps. The high number of repetitions necessitates that this attribute be worked on in training. Weight training is, because of the more efficient overload involved, more suited to developing this quality than simply rowing.

G. Here, the gymnast is executing an ``L'' iron cross, a superior strength move in still rings competition. The gymnast must possess tremendous strength in the muscles of the shoulder girdle as well as in the abdominal region. A case can be made for the necessity for the athlete to possess strength endurance as well, since the position must be held for a sustained period of time.

Methods of Muscular Endurance Development

While the keys to strength training and hypertrophy training are tension and variation, respectively, the key to muscular endurance training is oxygen utilization and transport. For these factors to become maximized, both the frequency and duration of the exercise must be high. The speed at which each repetition is to be performed should coincide, as nearly as possible, with the activity for which muscular endurance is sought, while the number of repetitions should not exceed forty or fifty (before the intensity of one's effort begins to decline). For example, a bicyclist, concerned about the leg muscles' capacity to continue sustained and repeated contractions during an all-out sprint race, or a swimmer, wishing to achieve local muscular endurance in the shoulder muscles for a 100-meter butterfly event, would, as closely as possible, approximate the speed at which their respective activities are performed during the weight training sessions. Further, in order to derive maximal benefit in this regard, sufficient weight would be used such that around forty or fifty repetitions could be performed at that speed. Dipping below the required speed would be analogous to slowing down a required speed in their respective sporting events. By training in this manner, overcompensation is forced on the muscles involved in the general capacity of that muscle to utilize oxygen, as well as in the circulatory system's capacity to deliver greater amounts of oxygen.

While little overlap is involved in mechanisms or methods employed in strength versus muscular endurance training, there is some evidence that the stronger a person is, the more likely that the muscular endurance will be high also. This statement makes reference to the difference between *absolute* endurance and *relative* endurance. If two people, one weak and the other strong, held a weight (say, 25 pounds) at arms' length, the stronger of the two would probably be capable of doing so for a longer period than the weaker. This is referred to as absolute endurance. In this case, strength and endurance are correlated highly. However, if each of the two were asked to perform the same exercise with a given percentage of their maximum capacity, such a correlation may alter, and we speak of each person's relative endurance. Notwithstanding this difference in terminology, from a purely practical point of view it would be to one's advantage to be strong, since in the real world of performance, absolute rather than relative differences are generally applied. While the stronger person would probably have more abundant stores of the high energy substrates ATP and phosphate creatine (PC), the more likely explanation of this phenomenon is that the protein troponin, which, as we saw earlier, is connected to the actin filaments for interaction with the calcium ions during contraction, becomes inactive as a result of increased acidity within the muscle fiber, thereby causing a decrement in that muscle's contractility. This increased acidity would not occur as quickly in the trained individual.

Factors Involved in Sporting Ability

The factors involved in sporting ability are many, and range in nature from the physiological to the psychological and sociological. Further, it seems necessary to point out that an athlete engaged in one sport may require completely different attributes than athletes in another sport, or even in the same sport but playing a different position. The following discussion, therefore, will be general; it is left up to the reader to ferret out those factors which he or she requires. Further, the list of factors discussed in this section by no means exhausts those which may be essential in sport; nor is it endemic to athletes. The general fitness enthusiast may find it helpful as well.

Before we proceed, however, there are some basic principles which should be considered by the athlete, regardless of the sport or activity engaged in. First, training regimen will vary during preseason, in-season, and off-season periods. Preseason training should be structured such that preparation for competition is the goal. Those attributes most directly involved in successful participation should be honed to a fine edge during this period. The length of the preseason training period should be generally low, not exceeding six to eight weeks. This is true because high-intensity training routines should be predominant; and should training in this manner continue longer, staleness or overtraining may result. High-intensity training generally involves applying greater and greater overload to the organism. For example, the sprint swimmer may reduce laps and increase speed per lap, the weight lifter may decrease repetitions and increase the amount lifted per repetition, or the long-distance runner may decrease the rest between intervals.

In-season training should be primarily concerned with maintenance of the factors trained for in the preseason and off-season. Power, for example, can be maintained by training only once or twice per week, performing maximal or near-maximal lifts. Should all training cease during the competition season, many of the hard-won gains will become diminished due to the law of use and disuse. Generally, one's actual activity does not offer sufficient overload to allow for maintenance of vital factors. Should the athlete continue to train three to six times weekly, on the other hand, the combined effect of training and competing may cause overtraining. Once or twice weekly is sufficient.

Off-season training regimen should be as broad as possible, incorporating all those factors deemed essential to adequate performance, and specifically those factors which appeared lacking during the competition season. A good coach may observe that the players (or individual player) lacked flexibility while performing their respective activities. The coach would, in the off-season training period, design and prescribe exercises specifically designed to increase flexibility. Research involving elite ice hockey players conducted at the University of Minnesota by Krotee, Alexander, and Chein suggests that definite programs of detraining closely related with physical activity level can be identified and adhered to in order to also maintain specific levels of cardiovascular endurance.

Throughout all seasons, skill requirements are generally attended to, although as stated previously, frequency, duration, and intensity of effort must be considered to alleviate staleness and overtraining. The preceding guidelines governing preseason, in-season, and off-season training regimen are not limited to weight training. They appear to be justifiable and appropriate in cases where little or no weight training is employed as well. Given the scope of this text, however, consideration is given only to weight training regimen.

All athletes must consider their specific activity's requirements. Having isolated them, the SAID, overload, and isolation principles must be applied in selecting and performing the appropriate exercises. The athlete requiring great power would be making a sad mistake to train for purely strength or local muscular endurance. Gains come slowly, and much time can be saved by prudent and judicious application of these principles. Correspondingly, the same athlete must consider those muscles involved in the specific event. For a sprinter to train upper body muscles exclusively, without training for leg power, would be ludicrous.

Power. While this factor has already been discussed in a preceding section, there are certain aspects which relate to sports that should be pointed out. As noted, speed and strength of contraction are the components of power. Some athletes (e.g., a quarterback) should accentuate the speed factor, while others (e.g., the lineman) should train more specifically for the explosive strength component. Such differential treatment of power exercises simply involves reductions or increases in the load such that the speed at which the respective athlete's activities are performed are closely approximated (at least 80%).

Hypertrophy. While athletes may not be interested in attaining a physique similar to a "Ms. or Mr. America," it is true that many sports require huge musculature for reasons of efficiency in performance. More importantly, however, strength and power are attained more easily once the appropriate amount of hypertrophy is attained. Gymnasts and wrestlers, together with many other athletes, place a premium on being light. However, they should nonetheless be muscular, keeping their body fat content to a minimum. Needless to say, nutrition plays an important role in such considerations, but nutrition alone cannot supply needed muscle tissue—only systematic training combined with sound nutritional practice can achieve that.

Speed. There still exists the myth that weight training (especially weight training for hypertrophy) is detrimental to sporting ability because speed and flexibility is impaired. As was discussed earlier in this chapter, speed can actually be facilitated through weight training, and increased muscular size may, in fact, add to that muscle's capacity to respond at maximum speeds. While somewhat unscientific, the analogy that the bigger the engine is, the more powerful it can be, applies.

Flexibility. Flexibility is defined as the ability of a joint to flex and extend through its full intended range of movement. Factors which may limit flexibility are many. Coaches speak of an athlete being "loose" or "tight" during performance. It has been suggested that tightness results from resistance of antagonistic muscles and their connective tissues. However, such a situation need not have been the result of weight training since, if anything, weight training would have "taught" the antagonists to relax during contraction of protagonists. This concept hinges on neuromuscular coordination, and repeated practice of a movement generally facilitates its development. In the case of weight training, there must be a two-way street in this process, however. In attempting to contract the tricep, which is the antagonist of the bicep, the same faciliatory response must have been practiced. Thus, in order to maintain flexibility in the joints acted upon by these muscles, both protagonists and antagonists must be exercised.

Impaired flexibility resulting from injury or genetic factors, or even from shortened muscles such as may occur from faulty posture or restricted movement can be improved through weight training. By strengthening the muscle which is antagonistic to the shortened (or injured) muscle, not only is the neuromuscular coordination improved, but the added pull by the strengthened muscle tends to offset the inordinate pull of the other.

Again, however, as in power, flexibility requirements may differ among different types of athletes. In fact, improved flexibility may be actually detrimental in some sports. The wise coach or athlete should identify his or her specific requirements in all factors influencing performance.

While weight training may be designed to facilitate flexibility, the standard method of static stretching must be considered as the most efficient method. Here, the muscle is stretched so that the stretch reflex (see Chapter 1) is bypassed via sustained pull, and the golgi tendon organ is stimulated to cause a general inhibition of contracture of the muscle under stretch. To facilitate this series of events, extreme concentration on relaxing the stretched muscle and holding the flexed position seven to twenty-five seconds seems to be helpful as well.

Skill. As was discussed, repetition of movements tends to increase both the precision as well as the efficiency of movement. Unnecessary contractures of antagonistic muscles tend to be decreased, and the desired movements become more automatic. Similarly, the amounts of energy substrate are significantly reduced due to the increased efficiency, thereby making the movements' costs, in terms of endurance, minimal. Since weight training tends to heighten the sensory stimulation (via the muscle spindles and golgi tendon organs) and to facilitate stimulation of appropriate motor units, skill, in the sense of the word described above, will be enhanced. It should be pointed out, however, that weight-training regimen designed for skill enhancement should be such that each exercise conforms exactly to the movements of the actual skill, both in pattern as well as speed. Only the amount of resistance should be increased. If the amount of weight is such that the speed of movement necessarily falls short of that at which the skill is normally performed, one should at least strive to keep the intensity of effort from faltering to the point of fatigue. Fatigue causes (often imperceptible) changes in the movement patterns being exercised, thereby rendering the athlete's efforts wasted or potentially detrimental.

Agility. Agility is the ability to exert a series of power vents (i.e., to change direction rapidly). As such, the same considerations as were discussed under speed and power should be adhered to. Another dimension which comes to bear in sporting performance of agility movements, however, is that of balance. Balance relates specifically to the location of one's center of gravity during stationary (static) or moving (dynamic) skills performances. Other than noting that a stronger, more powerful person can maintain required positions during static or dynamic skills, a detailed discussion of this attribute is beyond the scope of this text.

Endurance. Most coaches, and certainly most laymen, speak of endurance without regard for the differential mechanisms underlying it. Thus far in this text, differences between strength endurance and local muscular endurance were discussed, as were the methods of achieving them. Much current controversy exists as to whether weight training can contribute significantly to these types of endurance. While the mechanisms and methods of achieving cardiovascular (CV) and cardiorespiratory (CR) endurance are beyond the scope of this text (the reader is referred to one of the exercise physiology texts in the bibliography for in-depth coverage), the following guidelines should be helpful nonetheless.

As in local muscular endurance, which involves primarily aerobic capacity, CV and CR endurance is involved in oxygen transport and utilization. There are other parameters which come into play, however. *Maximum volume of oxygen uptake* (called Max$\dot{V}O_2$), or, the amount of oxygen consumption in the muscles, is due to (1) cardiac output, and (2) increased extraction of the oxygen from the blood at the muscles. Cardiac output generally depends on two not necessarily coincident factors, *heart rate,* (beats per minute) and *stroke volume* (amount of blood pumped out of the heart on each beat). Both appear to be somewhat related to the extraction factor (i.e., the extent of capillarization around the fibers). However, maximal stroke volume can be increased without a commensurate change in heart rate, and vice versa, simply because the trained heart, which can hypertrophy like any other trained muscle, becomes stronger, thereby more capable of pumping greater volumes of blood with each beat during strenuous exercise.

An increase in plasma volume is also noted after training. This effect serves to decrease blood viscosity, making it easier to flow through the tiny capillaries, thereby decreasing the cardiac work required. Hemoglobin (red, oxygen-carrying blood cells) count appears to be related to body size rather than to training effects, and increases in red blood cell count have not been conclusively linked with greater Max$\dot{V}O_2$ uptake capacity. Many athletes have, of late, used a method of *blood doping* to achieve greater endurance, a practice not entirely condoned nor proven efficacious. This practice involves the extraction of blood from the athlete weeks before a meet, and reinjecting it into the system just before the meet in the hopes that the increased hemoglobin count would give the athlete greater endurance capability.

While some training effect in respiratory efficiency is noted as a result of training, this effect appears to be limited to more efficient breathing patterns. This increased ventilation efficiency allows one to take in less air with heavy training, since the deeper breathing pattern more effectively ventilates the alveoli of the lungs (the tiny air sacs). Vital capacity (the amount of air one can breathe in), and the diffusing capacity of the lungs are thought to be unchanged as a result of training, and are more probably due to heredity.

Thus, it is clear that the locus for increased endurance resides primarily in the heart and muscles. Generally, nonrestrictive activities such as running will increase cardiac function more efficiently than will other, more restrictive exercises such as cycling or weight training. This is due to the fact that tension placed on the muscles restricts blood flow through the capillaries, thereby obviating the necessity of the heart to increase its stroke volume. In other words, recent evidence has been presented that indicates heart rate alone is not a sufficient situation to induce cardiac adaptation—stroke volume must be involved also.

Some weight-training methods are designed to maintain heart rates at or above 150 beats per minute, in the expectation that such a training regimen will yield cardiovascular as well as muscular benefits. There is some evidence that this is possible, in spite of a few conflicting reports. These training regimen, including *circuit training* and *interval training,* will be presented in the next chapter.

Long Range Effects of Physical Activity

As the authors strongly believe in a well-balanced program of individualized physical activity, the following long range effects occur when an individual participates in regular vigorous physical activity for a period of five to eight weeks. It is possible during this time for a training effect to occur. A training effect is a long range progressive adaptation or alteration of the body in response to participation in regular, vigorous physical activity. In general, improvements of up to 33% may occur in certain responses to vigorous participation in regular physical activity. The following training effects may occur after vigorous participation in a physical activity has been adhered to for a substantial time period:

Reduction in resting heart rate.

Reduction in resting pulse rate.

Reduction in resting blood pressure

Reduction in systolic blood pressure.

Increase in stroke volume.

Increase in cardiac output (stroke volume $\times$ heart rate).

Increase in coronary blood flow.

Decrease in the maximal heart rate attained during a standard work task.

A more rapid pulse rate response during work.

A more rapid recovery of the heart rate to resting level after physical activity.

Improved cardiovascular reflexes for mobilization of blood from the inactive to the active region of the body.

A lower level of fat content in the blood (cholesterol and triglycerides).

Increase in maximal oxygen uptake (the amount of oxygen consumed by the body per minute).

Increase in carbon dioxide output (per minute volume).

Increase in recovery of oxygen capacity or oxygen debt capacity.

Increase in lung capacity.

Reduction in pulmonary ventilation.

Lower blood lactate for a given amount of exercise.

Increase in muscular strength, fiber, and mass.

Increase in neuromuscular coordination.

Decrease in the amount of oxygen required for a standard work task.

Reduction in body fat and excess weight.

Increase in total hemoglobin.

Slight increase in the size of the heart and adrenal cortex.

Although there have been many claims ranging from the delaying of the onset of aging to the enhancement of sex life concerning the relative merits of regular participation in physical activity, none could be more vital than the possibility that participation in physical activity may reduce the incidence of cardiovascular disease. A review of the literature related to cardiovascular functioning suggests the following alterations may occur when the participant vigorously engages in a well designed program of physical activity for a sustained period of time:

Increase in the efficiency of the heart.

Increase in the coronary blood supply.

Development of collateral circulation (alternate blood vessels).

A reduced resting heart rate.

Increase in clearance of fat from the blood stream.

Reduction in the clotting ability of the blood.

Reduction in body fat and excess weight.

Reduction in systolic blood pressure.

It is these kinds of vital responses to physical activity that provide a possible explanation of why participation in regular, vigorous physical activity may be associated with reduction of incidence in cardiovascular disease and why physical activity should play an important role in the daily activity of every individual.

Notes on Legends, Stereotypes and Old Wives' Tales

Over the years, many beliefs concerning weight lifting, weight lifters, and what can and cannot be accomplished have been handed down not unlike fables and myths are. While many of these beliefs are based on fact, they are generally muddled to the extent that general comprehension of reality is impossible. Many, too, are based on personal experiences which have little to offer by way of objectivity. Many of these beliefs are presented in this section, with the ultimate goal of dispelling those which have no basis in fact, and shedding light on those which do.

Will weight training cause muscle-boundness? The belief that it does is probably the most widespread of the myths. As mentioned in the previous section, flexibility can actually be enhanced if one trains properly. Years ago, weight trainers may not have done so due to ignorance of many, possibly newly discovered, factors which are involved in weight training, and thereby may have become less flexible. Had the concepts of training antagonistic muscles and the proprioceptive mechanisms such as the muscle spindles and the golgi tendon organs been understood, this situation need never have occurred.

Can weight training improve cardiovascular fitness? Again, this problem was discussed in the previous section. It is generally agreed that in order for the heart to benefit from weight training, the heart rate must be kept above 150 beats per minute (BPM) for an extended period of time, generally for more than thirty minutes. While this can be accomplished in weight-training regimen, it is very difficult to do because of the intensity at which one must exercise. Further, there appears to be little gained in the vital area of stroke volume, due to the constriction of capillary blood flow in the exercised muscles. Probably the safest statement to make at this time is that weight training can be an invaluable adjunct to other systems of training which are more suited to increasing stroke volume along with maintenance of a high heart rate during exercise.

Are weight lifters dumb? The stereotype of the big, strong, lummox just off the farm comes to mind. This stereotype apparently stemmed from the formerly held belief that if athletes spent too much time in the gym, rather than in more scholarly pursuits, they would not become as learned as their non-weight lifting contemporaries. There is some evidence that, due to the high need-achievement found among most athletes involved in individual sports (including weight lifting), their pursuits off and on the gym floor are engaged in with success as a necessary goal. Therefore, one must conclude that weight lifters, like any other class of athletes, are at least average in intelligence, and may even experience greater levels of accomplishments than do their nonathlete contemporaries, again, possibly due to their high need for achievement. Many other psychosociological parameters can be considered here as well. Athletes, for example, tend to be more affiliative, more aggressive, less self-effacing, more managerial and less hostile than nonathletes. While these personality characteristics may or may not be significantly related to their IQ or learning capacity, a significant amount of research seems to indicate that many of the personality traits revered in our culture may be found in greater abundance among our sporting population.

Is weight lifting dangerous? Any competitive sport, when pursued on the championship level, can be dangerous. You are asking the body to perform at a level far above that which it is designed for. Football is the classic example, with far too many broken necks, injured knees and fractured fingers. Competitive weight lifting is no exception to this general rule. However, sport, if pursued for sports' sake or for fitness, is not necessarily dangerous. As has been discussed throughout the present chapter, weight training, when employed in the fashion mentioned, actually can prevent many of the injuries common in sports. Weight training is not dangerous, and if conducted in a scientific and safe manner (e.g., using spotters while performing heavy lifts), can be the difference between getting injured or staying healthy in sports. For further safety hints refer to the next chapter.

Do weight lifters' muscles turn to flab later in life? First of all, muscle tissue and fatty tissue are entirely different—one cannot become the other. Generally, athletes eat more during their active careers than most people, primarily due to their greater need for energy. Some athletes continue their eating habits even after dropping from competition, and as a result put on fat because their bodies no longer need the amount of calories they once did. Most, however, appear to remain relatively fit and trim long after their active years as athletes, probably because of reasons connected with their ego and self-image. Weight lifters are no exception to this rule. There are no reasons to believe that weight lifting, per se, contributes to obesity, and every reason to suspect otherwise.

Can one spot-reduce through weight training? For years vibrating machines and other assorted spot reducing gadgets have been associated with getting rid of those unwanted pounds of fat. Research, however, does not support the theory of spot reducing. There is a general adage among body builders regarding fat removal. Stated briefly, "last on, first off" or, "first on, last off." As calories are consumed in excess of the individual's daily energy requirements, fatty deposits accumulate, generally beginning around the midsection and upper hips, since these are the locations in closest proximity to the small intestines, where absorption of foodstuffs occurs. From there, deposits are made peripherally, gradually extending out to the limbs. While this course of events is an oversimplification in that one can develop fatty deposits peripherally before an enormous midsection is developed, it is nonetheless a useful guide in determining the extent to which one can reduce body fat concentrations. One cannot expect to lose fat in a localized area by exercising that area. It is the muscle tissue that is being exercised, and fat deposits are generally unaffected. Girth measurements can be reduced, however, but these reductions are probably due to the firming of underlying muscles rather than a real loss in fat. The best guide to follow in losing fat is to monitor your diet and engage in regular, vigorous physical activity. More will be said concerning nutrition in a following chapter.

Do women become overly muscled through weight training? Here, a value judgment is called for, regarding what constitutes feminine appearance. Only the extreme male chauvinist would lend credence to preconceived notions of femininity. The joy and exhilaration afforded the male in sports should be, and is, available to the female as well. Weight training is an integral part of the preparatory process in most sports, and women need the benefits of such training as much as men. Further, weight training for women is an excellent method of achieving fitness for the same reasons that it is so for men. There are obvious differences in what one can expect as outcomes, however. Men have greater supplies of the hormone testosterone than do women. This hormone is responsible for the greater capacity of the male to save nitrogen, necessary in the biosynthesis of muscle protein. This greater protein synthesis is what allows men to develop tremendous musculatures, and conversely, the lack of great amounts of testosterone in women generally negates this possibility. Needless to say, this aspect of masculinity-femininity can be represented by two overlapping distributions, a fact which explains why a few women have very masculine features and why a few men have relatively feminine features. On the whole, however, the great majority of women need never worry about becoming visually more muscular as a cross section of a muscle fiber can increase as much as 30% in diameter without measurable growth in the girth of an extended and relaxed body limb.

Before leaving the subject, however, one must consider what can be accomplished by women engaging in weight training programs. Women can expect to experience the same benefits as men in every instance—it is the degree of gain which will differ. Again, this difference in degree is relative to one's position within the respective overlapping distributions.

It should, however, be noted that once puberty is reached sex differences both cultural and genetic in nature do appear operational. The hormonal differences have been addressed in a previous section and seemingly the North American society has turned the corner in providing more equal and acceptable opportunity for women to participate in large muscle activities. An example of this is our university weight training and conditioning course offerings which indicate an equal number of men and women participants. Women do, however, seem to be at a disadvantage in some physiological measures. Women generally possess less muscle mass (23% vs. 40%), more fatty tissue resulting in higher average percent body fat (25% vs. 18%) measures, and possess less red blood cells as well as approximately 15% less hemoglobin (the protein and iron molecule that carries O_2 within the blood) which tend to reduce aerobic capacity. In our weight training classes women generally have averaged between 55%–65% strength capacity of that of the average man with the largest difference being in upper body (40%–50%) strength. With this in mind, the authors reaffirm that the benefit and relative gain in strength (see Strength Norm Charts located in the Progress Assessment Chapter) for women is for all practical purposes the same for men and in the case of the well trained female athlete the differences mentioned above seemingly diminish with the strength factor the lone possible exception.

Other characteristics such as greater bone density, larger joints, greater long bone measures, larger thoracic index, greater height, weight and heart size (stroke volume) measures fall in favor of the male, while the female possesses lower blood pressure (5–10 mm Hg), 5–10 BPM greater heart rate, 25% lower stroke volume output, a 10% lower vital capacity and a lower basal metabolic rate (BMR). These characteristics do exist but again the relative gain by women both physiologically and psychologically in regard to weight training seem to indicate equality.

Will weight training cause gynecological injury? It is now recognized that injuries to the female reproductive organs (which are well protected) are rare. Full participation during the pre-post menstrual cycle for those experiencing no discomfort should be encouraged, yet it should be recognized that this cycle does limit some individual's predisposition toward weight training.

Weight training is physical fitness. While weight training contributes to the strength component of physical fitness, the authors highly recommend that other components (cardiovascular endurance, flexibility, motor skill) be integrated for a well balanced program. Don't forget warm-up and cool-down!

Is weight training for adults only? Unfortunately United States children as well as adults fall well below the minimal level of physical fitness with strength (even one chin-up) being most evident. The fact that 10 million teenagers are **overweight** answers the question. Light weights, proper technique, safety and supervision are requisite for adolescent lifters!

Dehydration in the form of sweating will melt away the undesirable fat deposits. Dehydration resulting from steam baths, saunas, dry heat, and wearing a rubber suit (please avoid) will result in only temporary loss of water. After loss of 1% of your bodyweight in water you will most likely get thirsty and replace the lost fluid. After a loss of 3% of your body weight in water, research indicates that performance during physical activity will diminish. You can only lose weight (stored fat) by burning up calories, not by losing water weight. Care and caution is recommended when dealing with dehydration as your body should be able to dispel heat normally. Dehydration is also potentially dangerous for individuals with diabetes, heart disease, or high blood pressure.

Crash diets or starvation is a safe method of losing weight. Just as with dehydration, starvation may yield deleterious effects, including reduction in performance and cardiac efficiency. Crash diets, starvation, and dehydration are not recommended.

The amount of time that the participant engages in weight training is related to the increased possibility of losing weight. On the surface this statement is true; however, bear in mind that in order to lose one pound approximately 3,500 Kcal will have to be burned above your normal energy balance equation, resulting in a negative energy balance. During a positive energy balance, fat is synthesized in the liver and distributed for deposit, resulting in a gain in weight, but during a negative energy balance this fat is reclaimed for glycogen production. The intensity and duration of the physical activity, as well as your food intake, controls the possibility of losing or gaining weight.

Drinking water during physical activity will result in sickness and poor performance. Research indicates that "superhydrated" participants' work capacity appears not to be influenced. If you are thirsty, have a drink (a cup) of water! Milk has also been the target of study which has yielded that ingesting milk before engaging in physical activity does not have a detrimental effect on performance. It may also be noted that replacing lost water with fluids containing high concentrations of sugar or electrolytes that cannot be optimally absorbed by the intestinal system should be avoided.

Salt tablets assist in replacing lost salt during physical activity. Research indicates that you can lose up to six pints (6 lbs.) of water without needing salt replacement. If a salt tablet is taken (1 grain) it should be accompanied by two pints of water.

Carbohydrate or glycogen loading is an effective means of improving performance. Carbohydrate loading is the depletion of carbohydrate stores followed by an overloading of carbohydrates several days prior to physical activity. Research indicates that muscles may almost double their glycogen store which could improve performance in aerobic or endurance type physical activity. It must also be stated that carbohydrate loading has caused nausea and weakness, which may inhibit training prior to participation and should be experimented with only under proper professional supervision.

The best time to engage in weight training is in the early morning. Any time that it is convenient is the best time to engage in weight training!

Warm-up is of little or no value. Research indicates that general warm-up of the body musculature may influence performance from 1%–8% and that the muscles may maintain this heated state from 45–80 minutes. A good five minute general warm-up is recommended as a safety precaution for all participants engaging in regular, vigorous physical activity.

Fixed or blanket programs of physical fitness will enable me to reach my potential. It is recommended that set or fixed programs of fitness only be used as guides and ideas in the formulization of your own personalized weight training program. For those participants wanting to reach their potential it is recommended that well-trained medical and professional assistance be utilized to meet your specific needs, goals, aims, and desires.

In order to maintain fitness, you must engage in weight training at least five times per week. Research indicates that the participant need only train three to four times per week in order to develop a training effect. Training is the summation of adaptations induced by participation in regular (5–8 weeks), vigorous physical activity. Specificity of training refers to the particular physical activity you are in training for which in this instance is weight training. As the participant achieves a high level of fitness it is even possible to take off a few days without appreciably influencing the achieved fitness level.

Posture is related to health. This controversial topic has been the topic of conversation at every professional health meeting for decades. Poor posture is still believed to retard blood circulation. Specifically related to physical activity poor posture may place the participant in danger when performing various physical activity tasks, especially those involved with weight training.

The participant should allow for intensity and duration as well as technical changes when designing a weight training program. This statement may be true for those who wish to compete and have a "target" goal in mind which calls for peak performance during a certain time of the year (i.e., running the Boston Marathon). For these individuals a form of cyclic training is advisable. For those participants who have found a comfortable and enjoyable routine and want to continue maintaining the present level of fitness, the authors recommend that you continue with vigor and enthusiasm.

Engaging in weight training for the aged is a waste of time. Although some capacities do decrease when going through the aging process (i.e., protein synthesizing, muscular strength and endurance, cardiac output, and maximal heart rate), research indicates that well-controlled, regular physical activity can maintain and contribute to the functional capacity of the participant well into the later years. The older participant who engages in physical activity has the opportunity to exercise the same parameters as younger participants only not to as great an extent. The adage that you're not getting older, you're getting better certainly applies for those more experienced who continue to pursue physical activity through the life span.

You will never use ergogenic aids. Ergogenic aids consist of amphetamines, anabolic steroids, aspartic acid, and alkalies as well as caffeine, nicotine, alcohol, oxygen, hypnosis, loud noise, and even music! Chances are that you have succumbed to one of the above; however, it is the first few ergogenic aids on the list that the authors want you to recognize and avoid. Amphetamines (stimulants) may be addictive. They block signals of impending muscular fatigue and cause increase in heart rate and are thought to excite the nervous system as well as the respiratory system. The side effects are dizziness, confusion, eventual fatigue, and in some cases death from overdose. Amphetamines are dangerous and their use is unwarranted. Anabolic steroids draw the same recommendation. Steroids aid in retention of nitrogen necessary for the synthesis of protein allowing quick recovery from heavy exercise, which is related to building muscle mass.

Steroids have been found to be hepatic, carcinogenic, and responsible for undue edema and testicular shrinkage. Although still controversial as to their safety, the reader is strongly urged to avoid steroids. Aspartic acid in the form of potassium and magnesium is often related to the delay of fatigue. Research indicates that for the trained participant this delay in fatigue theory has not been supported, but in some instances it has been supported for the untrained. As aspartic acids are generally considered food and may be beneficial for some individuals, the authors recommend bananas! Alkalies in the form of sodium citrate and sodium bicarbonate have been experimented with because of their capacity to neutralize lactic acid, which accumulates in the blood as the waste product of the anaerobic pathway.

While it appears that physical work capacity may be increased, the side effects of possible nausea, stomach aches, diarrhea, and over excitability seem to outweigh the purported positive effects. Caffeine, nicotine, and alcohol simply treated retard coordination and have adverse effects on cardiovascular function. The authors further address ergogenic aids in the chapter concerning Nutrition for Health and Sport.

Summary

The astute reader has, by this time, realized that there are many different ways in which the overload factor can be manipulated. Listed in Figure 2.4 are some of the more common methods. Bear in mind, however, that there should be bounds within which the lifter must operate during overload, and these bounds are governed by his/her specific objectives, such as explosive strength (power), size, or muscular endurance. An example of these delimitations is presented in Figure 2.5. Reference to the key factors in each of these areas should remain of paramount concern to the lifter, regardless of his/her objectives. That is, in training for power, tension and speed are essential; in hypertrophy training it is variation of exercise regimen that will result in complete development; and in training for muscular endurance, one should be aware that oxygen transport and utilization are essential. Choosing the appropriate system of overload for each of these objectives will result in maximized gains in the shortest time possible. Finally, the SAID and isolation principles are vital to the efficient realization of personal objectives, and should therefore be incorporated along with appropriate overload.

Overload Manipulation Alternatives

---

1. Increasing the weight being lifted.

2. Increasing the speed of movement per repetition.

3. Stricter adherence to the isolation principle involving muscle groups.

4. Increasing the range of movement per repetition.

5. Increasing the duration of effort per repetition.

6. Increasing the number of sets and/or repetitions.

7. Minimizing the resting time between sets and/or repetitions.

8. Maximizing the activity level during rest periods by adding movement.

9. Increasing the number of physical activity sessions per day and/or week.

10. Adding additional movement patterns to the physical activity session.

Figure 2.4. Different methods of achieving overload in training. Adapted from Morehouse, Laurence E., and Miller, Augustus T., Jr.: *Physiology of Exercise,* ed. 7, St. Louis, 1976, The C. V. Mosby, Co.

Variable	Explosive Strength (Power)	Hypertrophy (Size)	Muscular Endurance
Load (% of maximum)	80-100	70-80	60-70
Duration (seconds per set)	5-10	30-40	90-120
Repetitions per Set	3-5	10-15	40-50
Sets per Exercise	3-4	4-6	2-4
Rest between Sets (minutes)	3-4	4-5	1-2
Speed per Repetition (% of optimal)	90-100	80-90	70-80
Physical Activity Sessions per Week (frequency)	3-4	5-6	10-14

Figure 2.5. Prescribed methods of overload for power, size, and muscular endurance. Adapted from Morehouse, Laurence E., and Miller, Augustus T., Jr.: *Physiology of Exercise,* ed. 7, St. Louis, 1976, The C. V. Mosby Co.

Preparation for Weight Training

3

The Development of Aims and Objectives

In order to gain optimal benefit from participation in any activity, it may be best to develop sound rationale (aims and objectives) for what you are attempting to accomplish. Participation in regular, (3–4 times/week) vigorous weight training can be enjoyable and challenging but it requires hard work, time, and dedication. With this focus in mind the following list of behavioral objectives are meant to serve as a framework from which each participant should identify, modify, and further develop a more detailed and more personalized set of aims, objectives, and expected outcomes in order to meet your fitness needs and desires.

1. To develop the physical and organic self.

   To reverse the trend of physical inactivity.

   To develop muscular strength.

   To develop muscular endurance.

   To develop cardiovascular endurance.

   To develop coordination and body control.

   To develop knowledge and understanding concerning the physical and organic self.

   To develop knowledge, understanding, and awareness concerning the relationship between the structure and function of the body and psychosocial self.

   To develop a safe and individualized program of weight training appropriate for the participant's specific needs, fitness level, and potential.

2. To develop physical and neuromuscular skill.

   To learn the basic locomotor skills.
      Skills such as lifting, swinging, climbing, rolling, pushing, and pulling.

   To learn the basic nonlocomotor skills.
      Skills such as stretching, twisting, bending, and proper postural alignment.

To learn the basic sport and recreational skills.

Skills specifically related to the above, such as power weight lifting, Olympic weight lifting, and recreational weight training.

To acquire knowledge and understanding concerning safe participation in weight training within the limits of the participant's physical and neuromuscular potentialities.

3. To develop various psychosocial qualities as related to weight training.

To develop a positive attitude.

To develop knowledge and understanding concerning the values of participation in weight training and their relationship to physical, mental, and emotional health.

To develop an outlet for self-expression and creativity.

To develop an aesthetic appreciation for the wide spectrum of weight training and its associated surroundings.

To develop various psychosocial qualities such as self-control, discipline, self-confidence, self-esteem, body image, initiative, poise, and other associated factors pertaining to the total growth and development of the psychosocial self.

There seem to be many factors which serve to motivate individuals to engage in regular, vigorous weight training. Whether your objective is to maintain over-all muscle tone, improve local muscular endurance and strength, increase flexibility, maintain proper body weight and size, aid in recovery from an injury, prevent injury, prepare for a sport specific task, or just acquire personal satisfaction and enjoyment, these aims and objectives, both short range and long range in scope, should be committed to paper. The resulting training program should also be periodically assessed, evaluated, and reshaped in order to facilitate you in reaching your personalized fitness goals. Daily logs of your workout regimen and training gains as well as your nutritional intake should be accurately recorded in order to assess your progress. You will find your progress a pleasant surprise and this will serve as an additional motivator to an already enjoyable personal process on the way to improving your quality of life.

Safety Considerations

Although weight training is one of the safest forms of physical activity in which you will participate, any time you engage in physical activity that is meant to enhance the quality of life, it may not always be completely risk free.

The more sedentary and closer the participant is to age 30, the more you should be aware that a thorough medical examination, including an exercise stress test, by a qualified physician is requisite. For the apparently healthy participant this examination procedure will serve to indicate possible latent ischemic heart disease that may not be noticeable during a sedentary physical examination. The test may also serve as a barometer and further motivating force for you to participate in regular, vigorous activity of which weight training should be an integral segment.

In addition to receiving a medical examination and exercise stress test by competent medical personnel, other precautions and considerations are required in order to maximize your safety, the safety of others, and ensure an enjoyable experience in weight training. The following are recommended guidelines:

1. Never train alone! Injuries and accidents can often be avoided when someone else is present. It's also more fun to involve others either as a primary or secondary partner. A weight training room should be supervised by trained personnel.

2. Inspect equipment, read instructions and have each piece of equipment demonstrated by a qualified instructor. In short, if you don't know what you're doing, seek professional advice and guidance. Your chances of reaching your training aims and objectives will be greatly enhanced.

3. Use experienced spotters whenever necessary. Heavy squats and bench presses are especially dangerous and under no circumstances should they be attempted without one or two knowledgeable spotters. Other exercises such as good mornings, hyperextensions, and incline or decline presses also require spotting.

4. Keep alert and lift weights or engage in associated physical activity in designated areas only. With multi-use equipment be aware of where you are as well as others around you. Be careful not to walk directly in front of lifters as you may startle them, disturb their concentration, or even inadvertently bump into their equipment.

5. Always check your weights and immediate training environment before each set. Be sure that even loading is followed, collars are tightened and barbell sleeves are free to revolve. Count your weight!

6. Use equipment as it was designed to be employed. Improper use can cause injury, equipment breakdowns, and lost training time.

7. Keep lifting and exercise areas clean, neat, and orderly. Place weights in designated areas after using, as misplaced weights are often the cause of injury.

8. When using weight training machines, carefully check all cables, pulleys, selector keys, (use appropriate key not a substitute), nuts, bolts, cam chains, seat adjustments and belts for maximum safety. The equipment should also be kept clean and appropriately lubricated. If equipment jams, do not attempt to free it yourself. Report all problems immediately to the weight training supervisor.

9. Wear proper lifting attire and remember perspiration causes slippery equipment and skin, both dangerous conditions. Don't lift in your stocking feet! (See equipment)

10. Use proper breathing techniques when lifting. Rhythmic breathing technique (exhale when lifting) is recommended to avoid breath holding which is associated with the valsalva maneuver.

11. Don't lift if an injury may be aggravated. Temporarily modify the activity to exclude the injured area or associated muscle group.

12. If you're not feeling well or even up to par, you should temporarily suspend lifting. When recovering from an illness, resume lifting at a level of intensity and weight level well below that achieved before the illness.

13. Attend to weight training through a planned personalized program of progressive resistance training. This will reduce muscle soreness, aching joints and tendons and reduce your chance for injury. Proper technique, supervision in a professionally developed weight training program is mandatory.
14. Be aware of environmental conditions such as room temperature, humidity, altitude, and pollution count and adapt your weight lifting program accordingly.
15. Don't lift immediately after a heavy meal!
16. Excessively hot showers should be avoided immediately after training. In some rare instances, hot showers have been associated with manifestations of myocardial infarction or heart attack.
17. Weight training does not have to be highly competitive in nature to be healthful. In fact, ego in the form of spontaneous and unwarranted 1-RM's like trying to outlift a colleague often leads to a loss of safety focus concerning the physiological boundaries for safe participation.
18. As part of the physiological and psychological preparation for weight training, the warm-up may be considered a safety precaution. Warm-up is a preparation that is conducted at submaximal effort for a duration of approximately five to fifteen minutes immediately before engaging in lifting. Warm-up should be intense enough to increase body temperature and cause perspiration, but should not require a longer duration of submaximal effort. The value of warm-up seems to be quite controversial for participation in various sport specific situations; however, for the individual engaging in regular, vigorous weight training, warm-up is deemed as a vital safety factor.

The physiological and psychological value of warming up before engaging in weight training are thought to include the following:

1. Helps prevent injury to muscles, tendons, and ligaments.
2. Increases the temperature of the muscle and blood, thereby positively affecting oxygen utilization.
3. Increases the heart rate and blood pressure.
4. Increases maximal oxygen uptake.
5. Increases circulation.
6. Increases joint mobility.
7. Increases the speed and force of muscular contraction.
8. Reduces pulmonary blood flow resistance in the lungs.

Warm-up usually includes a combination of preliminary exercise including light calisthenics, jogging, stationary cycling (5 minutes), loosening of the muscles and static stretching (5 minutes), a brief task specific activity such as practicing lifting techniques employing low level weight 20%–50%/1-RM (5 minutes) and a tapering off period of three to five minutes depending on the type of personalized weight training program to be followed that day. The psychological value of warm-up is at this writing not clearly understood; however, mental preparation, concentration, mental rehearsal, and visual imagery are most often mentioned in the research literature. Mental preparation, preparatory set, and the readiness and awareness to participate are certainly important factors in safe and successful participation in regular, vigorous weight training.

Besides the recommended warm-up period, another critical part of safe participation is the "cooling down" period. The "cooling down" period should follow immediately after the main bout of weight training and usually is confined to submaximal or low intensity bodily movement such as jogging, walking, swimming, and static stretching. The importance of the cooling down period is to allow the muscles to divert the blood which has been distributed to the various extremities of the body back to the vital organs. If the extremity muscle contraction is abruptly stopped, the blood may pool and occasionally light headedness or black out could occur. It is recommended that a five-minute cooling down period be adopted after each exercise bout before retiring to the locker room.

General Lifting Guidelines and Tips

1. Set weekly, monthly, and yearly goals. Write them down and maintain accurate records.
2. Exercise 3–4 times per week for at least 30–60 minutes.
3. Employ 8–16 (average 12) types of exercise modes alternating body regions and muscle groups.
4. Use proper techniques at all times utilizing *compensatory acceleration* during the complete range of motion with such exercises as squats, bench presses, cleans and high pulls. Simply stated get the most out of each repetition by completing that motion as hard as possible until just before exercise termination.
5. Don't try to impress others! Stick to your personalized program.
6. Use rhythmic breathing inhaling as the weight is lowered and generally exhaling as the weight is lifted. Do not hold your breath!
7. Exercise from large muscle groups to smaller ones.
8. The duration of each lift should proximate 2.5–4.0 seconds.
9. Most exercises require the feet to be shoulder width apart and toes pointed slightly (20°) outward. Always maintain balance!
10. Don't squeeze the grips, but do maintain a firm grip with dry hands.
11. Keep body properly aligned especially the back for maximal safety and efficiency.
12. Remember to warm-up, cool down and avoid any "trouble" exercises such as full squats or hyperextensions if you have knee or back problems.
13. Always check equipment before lifting.
14. See your teacher, coach, or weight training specialist if your program does not seem comfortable or challenging. All programs must be altered as to intensity, duration, and frequency as progress dictates moving toward your next phase of cyclic training.

Common Injuries

Unfortunately, engaging in vigorous weight training may cause slight, temporary pain and discomfort due to the occurrence of minor injury. Below are a list of some of the injuries that are commonly associated with weight training.

Muscle Soreness—Occasionally vigorous weight training is followed by some degree of muscular soreness or stiffness. This may be avoided to some extent by beginning lifting at a low level of muscular exertion and progressing in gradual stages. Warm-up may also aid

in reducing this type of minor ailment. Keeping warm after weight training is also recommended. If muscle soreness does occur, light exercise, massage or warm (95°F–104°F)
whirlpool may be employed. Weight training should be suspended if the injury requires
rest. Muscle soreness is associated with ruptured muscle fiber, torn or strained connective
tissue as well as muscular spasm.

Blister or Torn Callus—Blisters are caused by heat and friction. Prevention is the best treatment and gloves, hand grips, and carbonate magnesium are often utilized in this regard.
Blisters may be punctured leaving on the skin, drained, antibiotic ointment applied, kept
clean and covered during lifting. Callus may be shaved off using an emery board.

Sprains—A sprain is a tear, rupture, or marked stretching of a capsule or ligament of a joint.
The sprain may range from acute (local hemorrhage and swelling from sudden excess use)
to chronic (overuse associated with pain and limitation of motion). Grade I and II or first
and second degree sprains need only protection and rest until healing; however, Grade III
or third degree injury does result in joint instability. Rest, elevation, ice within twenty-four
hours, and firm wrapping are recommended and then REST.

Strains—A strain is pain in a muscle-tendon unit due to excessive stretching or overuse. Most
strains are minor in nature but major in pain production and occur as a result of improper
lifting techniques. Rest, heat, and relaxation are recommended until healing permits returning to training.

Hyperextension—Hyperextension means to over straighten and is often caused by lifting too
much weight and using poor lifting technique. Back raises, good morning exercises, elevated pulls, back hyperextensions, as well as all lifting exercises associated with the neck
area deserve great *CAUTION*. Warm-up and progressive build up must be especially observed!

Tendonitis—Inflammation of the tendon approximate to the joint is called tendonitis. The most
common areas for tendonitis include the biceps, elbow, knee, and of course the Achilles
area. Rest is recommended with heat and massage until the injury is healed.

Bursitis—Bursitis is an inflammation of a bursa or sac that is associated with the joint. It is
most common around the shoulder region. Rest is recommended.

Other Injuries—Other injuries more serious in nature often associated with heavy lifting include muscle tears or separations, rotator cuff injury, chondromalaia or softening of the
cartilage (usually about the knee), herniation, epicondylitis or inflammation of the elbow,
and pinched nerves. These are not, however, common injuries for the prudent and regular
vigorous weight trainer and may be thought as representative of destructive overload in
regard to serious weight training practice.

In summary, you can expect your weight training experience to be enjoyable, safe, and
relatively risk free if you adhere to the principles of weight training and attend to the safety
considerations and general weight training guidelines and tips presented by the authors.

Equipment for the Lifter

Participation in weight training unlike engaging in some forms of physical activity is relatively uncumbersome in regard to equipment needs. For the purpose of this text a brief list of
recommended weight training equipment from head to toe is presented.

Head or Sweat Bands—Bands are used to keep hair and cranial perspiration in check.

Sweat or Heavy T-shirt—Shirts are requisite for weight room safety and cleanliness. The shirts serve to keep body perspiration in check thereby keeping perspiration to a minimum when moving from bench to machine. Heavy shirts also serve as shoulder pads, protection, and non-skid surface for equipment that is placed on the shoulders during squatting or other shoulder press related exercises.

Breast Support

Sweat Pants—Sweat pants are recommended for perspiration control as well as for their non-slip factor. Brief shorts usually do not allow for enough range of motion and are inadequate covering for the crotch area during bench exercises. The more flexible synthetic fabrics seem more suitable for shorts than cotton varieties.

Leotards—Leotards seem fine for coverage but do not absorb perspiration as well as sweat pants.

Belts—Weight belts are frequently seen in weight rooms but are relatively unnecessary unless lifting extremely heavy weights. Exercising without the added support of a belt allows both the muscles of the abdominal and back regions to accept the stress of exercise thereby allowing them to become more developed. The utilization of the belt would otherwise "rob" these muscles of the opportunity to become stronger. However, when the weights being lifted (particularly in overhead and squatting movements) become so heavy that only five repetitions can be performed, then the belt is recommended for safety. The belt will support the abdominal region when squatting and prevent the spine from flexing or moving forward. The belt will also serve to prevent spinal hyperextension during the overhead movements. Correct lifting posture is vital during all forms of weight lifting!

Athletic Supporter

Women's Athletic Brief

Gloves—Gloves will protect the hands from becoming blistered or overly callused. A tight fitting pair of handball gloves serves the purpose as well as any. There are weight training gloves on the market that are very effective and safe as well. Gloves are recommended in weight training facilities that provide no carbonate magnesium (chalk) for hand perspiration. Sweaty hands may cause the bar to slip from the lifter's grasp, and can be quite dangerous. If neither chalk nor gloves are at hand a towel should be mandatory both to avoid sweaty hands as well as to keep the equipment dry.

Hand Grips—Canvas or leather type material "grips" are often used for holding the bar in the hands. One end of the grip encircles the wrists while the other wraps around the bar, with the weight of the bar holding the straps against the palm of the hand, thereby preventing the bar from slipping from the grasp. Grips are recommended for lifting heavy weights (particularly in the bent row, deadlift, or upright row movements), but should never be used when lifting the bar overhead by anyone other than highly experienced lifters. This is because the bar may be held to the hand so well that it cannot be quickly released, causing severe shoulder or elbow injury if the bar is dropped. Olympic weight lifters use hand grips in overhead movements, but have become experienced at it, and have learned how to rid themselves of the bar if they inadvertently drop the bar from an overhead position.

Supportive Clothing or Devices—Powerlifters and Olympic weight lifters commonly use knee or wrist wraps to prevent injury and/or to assist in supporting heavier weights while in competition. In training, when extremely heavy weights are being used, such supportive devices can often mean the difference between getting injured or not. However, in typical weight training circumstances, knee and wrist wraps are not recommended for the same reason belts are not. They tend to "rob" the supportive muscles of the opportunity of receiving adaptive stress, and therefore the chance to become stronger. In recent years, competing powerlifters have begun using highly supportive "girdle-like" suits that allow them to lift as much as thirty to fifty pounds more in the squat movement. This is within the limits of the rules of the sport, and it is done for the reason of achieving as high a total as possible, but is not recommended for the average weight trainer whose efforts should be directed towards building a solid foundation of strength and muscle size rather than seeing how much they can lift in a competitive or ego-gratifying sense.

Socks

Training Shoes—Training shoes are available on the market and would make a valuable contribution to the safety of weight lifting as many free weight injuries still involve injured toes. Training shoes with wide flat sole support are adequate as compared to narrow running shoes. Balance and stability are critical when lifting!

Schedule and Pencil—Don't forget your workout schedule and pencil to record your daily, weekly, and monthly progress.

Weight Training Equipment Companies and Resources

Weight Training Equipment Companies

The following list of weight training companies was compiled to give the reader an idea of the various equipment manufacturers and outlets. Although far from complete it gives the weight trainer an idea of the professional companies operating within your interest area.

Adonis Fitness Equipment
960 North Street
Tweksbury, Maryland 01876
(617) 851–6340

AMF American Athletic Equipment
200 American Avenue
Jefferson, Iowa 50129
(515) 386–3125

Askew's Body Building Equipment
8023 S.E. 17th
Portland, Oregon 97203
(503) 233–4183

Atlantis HiTech Fitness Systems
1685 38th Street
Boulder, Colorado 80301
(303) 447–2091

Bell Foundry Co.
5310 Southern Avenue
South Gate, California 90280
(213) 564–5701

Body Culture Gym Equipment (Eleiko)
Box 10
Alliance, Nebraska 69301

Body Masters
P.O. Box 259
Rayne, Louisiana 70578
(318) 934–0319

Champion Barbell Mfg. Company
Box 1507
Arlington, Texas 76010

Corbin-Gentry, Inc.
40 Maple Street
Somersville, Connecticut 06072
(800) 243–5728

Cybex
3100 W. Calhoun Boulevard
Minneapolis, Minnesota 55416
(800) 645–5382

Diversified Products
309 Williamson Avenue
Opelika, Alabama 36802

Eagle Performance Systems
2030 South Cedar
Owatonna, Minnesota 55060
(507) 455–0217

Fitness International
P.O. Box 39696
Phoenix, Arizona 85069

Fitness Research Institute/Body Building
2210 Wilshire Boulevard
Suite 753
Santa Monica, California 90403

Fitness Store
5324 Excelsior Boulevard
St. Louis Park, Minnesota 55416

Fitness Systems U.S.A.
3335 St. Charles Avenue
New Orleans, Louisiana 70130

G. B. Manufacturing Company
206 E. Water Street
Sandusky, Ohio 44870

Gary Schroeder Sports Inc.
514 4th Avenue
Long Prairie, Minnesota 56347

Global Fitness Equipment
2075 Sparta Court
Olympia Fields, Illinois 60461

Gopher Athletic
County Road #45 North
Owatonna, Minnesota 55060

Hoggan Health Equipment Inc.
6651 South State
Salt Lake City, Utah 84107

Hydra-Gym Inc.
2121 Industrial Boulevard
Belton, Texas 76513
(800) 433–3111

Iron Company
5334 Banks Street
San Diego, California 92110
(714) 278–1440

Josef Schnell
8898 Peutenhausen
Sportweg 9, West Germany

Jubinville Health Equipment
P.O. Box 662
Holyoke, Massachusetts 01041

Keiser Sports Health Equipment
411 South West Avenue
Fresno, California 93706
(209) 266–2715

Leflar
6840 S.W. Macadam
Portland, Oregon 97219
(503) 246–7784

Magnum Exercise Equipment Inc.
8222 Jamestown Drive
Austin, Texas 78758

Marcy Fitness Products
2801 West Mission Road
Alhambra, California 91800
(213) 570–1222

Mav Rik
3916 Eagle Rock Boulevard
Los Angeles, California 90665
(213) 257–9139

MGI Inc. (Mini Gym)
P.O. Box 266
909 W. Lexington
Independence, Missouri 64050

Muscle Dynamics
17022 Montanero Street
Carson, California 90746

Nautilus Sports/Medical Industries
P.O. Box 1783
DeLand, Florida 32720
(904) 228–2884

Nordic Exercise Equipment
Ala Moana Boulevard
Honolulu, Hawaii 96813

Olympic Enterprises
1333 North 22nd Avenue
Phoenix, Arizona 85009

Paramount Health Equipment Corp.
3000 South Santa Fe Avenue
Los Angeles, California 90058
(800) 421–6242

Pitt Barbell
126 Penn Hills Mall
Pittsburgh, Pennsylvania 15235

Polaris Conditioning Equipment
5334 Banks Street
San Diego, California 92110
(619) 297–4349

Power Body Building
1101 N.E. Stinson Boulevard
Minneapolis, Minnesota 55413

Professional Gym Inc.
805 Cherokee
Marshall, Missouri 65340
(816) 886–3042

Prostar Sports Inc.
2300 West Hwy. 40
Blue Springs, Missouri 64015

Questar
233 Wilshire Boulevard
Santa Monica, California 90401

Rocky Mountain Gym
5745 Monaco Street
Commerce City, Colorado 80022

Saf-T-Gym
815 Alexander Valley Road
Healdsburg, California 95448

Sisco Company
Box 12096
Knoxville, Tennessee 37912

Ultra Performance Systems
10150 W. Nimbus Avenue
E-2 Koll Business Center
Tigard, Oregon 97223
(503) 684–1480

Universal-Nissen
P.O. Box 1270
Cedar Rapids, Iowa 52406
(800) 553–7901

Weider Health and Fitness
21100 Erwin Street
Woodland Hills, California 91367
(800) 423–5713

World Class Gym Equipment
2602 South Oak
Santa Ana, California 92707
(714) 546–4913

York Barbell Company
P.O. Box 1707
York, Pennsylvania 17405

Exercise Equipment Summary Chart

The chart (pp. 55–57) is designed to give those interested in weight training a view of the various types of equipment on the market. The list is by no means complete and contains only a sample of representative weight training equipment companies and manufacturers. It is not the role of the authors to impose professional judgments as to the attractiveness, durability, quality of construction including brushing, bearings, welds, machinery, metals used, and upholstery, and to its versatility including the performance and cost ratio of the exercise equipment presented. However, the above elements as well as others must be addressed when considering high quality strength and fitness training. Requisite to the chart, the equipment should allow for the following: 1) multiple joint exercise, 2) ballistic movement under controlled circumstances, 3) adjustments in movement pattern and biomechanical advantage, 4) great variation in strength, size of the lifter and 5) enable the weight trainer to perform sport specific weight training tasks.

Few machines are fully capable of meeting the above criteria, so naturally these authors advocate the use of free weights for most serious sport related lifters. Space age technology, however, is rapidly moving to design weight training machines that will safely serve to meet the needs of the novice through expert weight trainers. These advances will provide even greater opportunity to improve our quality of life through personalized strength training and fitness.

Weight Training Facility and Design

The diagram (p. 58) is meant to be a design of a model 40 × 64 weight training facility with accompanying equipment list. The facility is designed with the concept of total fitness in mind with ample aerobic fitness (stationary bikes, treadmills, rowing and nordic ski machines) and stretching areas included in its design as well as plate holders (P) and dumbbell racks. The checked pattern denotes special rubberized tiles designed to absorb the shock and noise of the free weight area. The design, of course, is just a conceptual framework from which to create a functional training facility to meet your institutions', community, or sport specific teams', personalized weight training and physical fitness needs.

Equipment List

A. Selectorized Machines
  1. Universal Power Pak 200 (2)
  2. Universal Knee and Thigh
  3. Paramount Leg Extension Leg Curl (Uniflex)
  4. Hoggan Quad Pulley Machine
  5. Universal Long Pull
  6. Universal Seated Lat Pull
  7. Universal Wall Mount High Pulley
  8. Universal or World Class Crossover Pulley Machine
  9. Nautilus Super Pullover Machine
  10. Paramount Uniflex Chest Press
  11. Paramount Seated Butterfly (Pec Deck)
  12. Eagle Performance Systems Rotory Torso

B. Plate Loading Machines (Olympic)
  1. Universal Power Leg
  2. Universal Smith Machine
  3. Universal Standing Calf
  4. Universal Seated Calf
  5. Universal Olympic Lever Bar

C. Free Weights
1. York or Ivanko 400 lb. Olympic Sets (6 sets)
2. York or Ivanko 45 lb. Olympic Plates (14 pairs)
3. York or Ivanko 25 lb. Olympic Plates (6 pairs)
4. Askew Fixed Weight Dumbbells (Paramount for 2, 4, 6, 8 lbs.)
5. Paramount 5 Pair Dumbbell Racks (5)
6. Askew Fixed Weight Barbells (20–115 lbs.) (20)
7. Askew or Cal Gym Fixed Weight Barbell Rack
8. AMF E-Z Curl Olympic Bars (2)

D. Benches and Apparatus
1. Askew Power Rack
2. AMF Squat Stool
3. AMF Adjustable Olympic Supine Press Bench
4. Universal Olympic Incline Press Bench
5. Custom Made Chin Bar
6. Nissen 3 Station Chrome Stall Bars
7. Paramount Flat Abdominal Board with Strap
8. Paramount Knee Rest Abdominal Board with Strap
9. Paramount Knee Rest Abdominal Board with T-Bar
10. Askew Hip Flexor and Dip Station
11. Universal Dip Station
12. Askew Back Extension Apparatus
13. Askew Adjustable Incline Benches (2)
14. Askew Custom Tapered Bench
15. Askew Flat Benches (3)
16. Universal Seated Preacher Curl Stand
17. Universal Multi-Purpose Exercise Bench
18. Askew Narrow Grip Supine Press Bench
19. Muscle Dynamics Adjustable Decline Bench
20. Custom Made Analysis and Exercise Table
21. Muscle Dynamics Behind the Neck Press Bench
22. Universal Vertical Weight Racks (10)
23. Universal Horizontal Olympic Weight Racks (2)
24. Custom Made Chalk Boxes (2)

E. Stationary Progressive Resistance Machines and Equipment
1. Monarch Exercise Bikes (2)
2. Schwinn Exercise Bikes (2)
3. Tenturi Exercise Bike (1)
4. Fitron Exercise Bike (1)
5. Haden Treadmill
6. Quinton Treadmill
7. Trotter Treadmill
8. Nordic Ski Machine
9. Rowing Machine

Of course this is only a partial list and for more information concerning design, construction, or equipment it is suggested you contact any of the resource consultants listed on p. 59.

Exercise Equipment Summary Chart

Company	Selectorized: Chrome—Solid machined steel	Selectorized: Chrome—welded tubing	Selectorized: Painted—welded tubing	Plate-loading: Chrome—welded tubing	Plate-loading: Painted—welded tubing	Benches Racks Apparatus: Chrome—machined solid steel	Benches Racks Apparatus: Chrome—welded tubing	Benches Racks Apparatus: Painted—welded tubing	Free Weights: Olympic—Kilos	Free Weights: Olympic—Pounds	Free Weights: Dumbbells—Chrome	Free Weights: Dumbbells—Black	Free Weights: Dumbbells—Fixed	Resistance Mode: Isotonic—Standard	Resistance Mode: Dynamic—Variable	Resistance Mode: Isokinetic—Fixed	Resistance Mode: Isokinetic—Variable	Resistance Mode: Air/Water/Friction	Single Station Only	Single & Multiple Station
Adonis Fitness Equip. 960 North Street Tewksbury, MA 01876			X					X						X	X				X	X
AMF (515) 386–3125 200 American Avenue Jefferson, IA 50129					X		X	X		X		X	X	X					X	
Askew Body Building Equip. (503) 233–4183 8023 S.E. 17th Portland, OR 97203						X		X		X		X	X						X	
BFCO (213) 564–5701 5310 Southern Avenue South Gate, CA 90280										X		X		X						
Body Culture Equip. (Eleiko) Box 10 Alliance, NB 69301									X					X						
Body Masters (318) 984–0319 Box 259 Rayne, LA 70578			X												X				X	

Continued

Exercise Equipment Summary Chart

Company	Selectorized: Chrome—Solid machined steel	Selectorized: Chrome—welded tubing	Selectorized: Painted—welded tubing	Plate-loading: Chrome—welded tubing	Plate-loading: Painted—welded tubing	Benches/Racks/Apparatus: Chrome—machined solid steel	Benches/Racks/Apparatus: Chrome—welded tubing	Benches/Racks/Apparatus: Painted—welded tubing	Free Weights: Olympic—Kilos	Free Weights: Olympic—Pounds	Free Weights: Dumbbells—Chrome	Free Weights: Dumbbells—Black	Free Weights: Dumbbells—Fixed	Resistance Mode: Isotonic—Standard	Resistance Mode: Dynamic—Variable	Resistance Mode: Isokinetic—Fixed	Resistance Mode: Isokinetic—Variable	Resistance Mode: Air/Water/Friction	Single Station Only	Single & Multiple Station
Corbin-Gentry, Inc. (800) 243–5728 40 Maple St. Sommersville, CT 06072					X										X				X	
Eagle Performance Systems (800) 455–0217 2030 South Cedar Owatonna, MN 55060		X	X							X					X					
Global Fitness Equip. Inc. 2075 Sparta Court Olympic Fields, IL 60461		X												X	X					X
Hoggan Health Equip. 6651 South State Salt Lake City, UT 84107	X					X					X			X						X
Hydra-Gym Inc. (800) 433–3111 2121 Industrial Rd. Belton, TX 76513			X													X	X	Air		X
Iron Co./Polaris Equip. Co. 5334 Banks St. San Diego, CA 92110			X					X		X	X	X	X		X				X	
Ivanko P.O. Box 1470 San Pedro, CA 90733										X	X	X	X	X						

Manufacturer																		
Josef Schnell 8898 Peutenhausen Sportweg 9, West Germany										X								
Keiser Sports Hlth Equip. 411 So. West Avenue Fresno, CA 93706																X	X (Air)	X
MGI Mini Gym P.O. Box 266, 909 Lexington Independence, MO 64050		X							X						X	X (Frict.)		
Marcy Fitness Products 2801 West Mission Road Alhambra, CA 91800		X		X		X			X			X	X	X				X
Mav-Rik (213) 275–9139 3916 Eagle Rock Blvd. Los Angeles, CA 90665						X												
Nautilus Sports Medical P.O. Box 1783 DeLand, FL 32720		X	X									X				X		
Paramount Health Equip. 3000 South Santa Fe Ave. Los Angeles, CA 90058	X	X	X	X	X	X	X	X	X		X	X	X	X	X			X
Ultra Performance Systems 10150 W. Nimbus Avenue Tigard, OR 97223			X					X				X	X	X	X (Water)			X
Universal-Nissen P.O. Box 1270 Cedar Rapids, IA 52406		X	X	X		X			X		X	X	X	X				X
Weider Health & Fitness 21100 Erwin Street Woodland Hills, CA 91367						X		X			X (sets)	X						
World Class Gym 2602 South Oak Santa Ana, CA 92707		X		X		X			X		X	X	X	X				X
York Barbell Co. P.O. Box 1707 York, PA 17405							X	X										

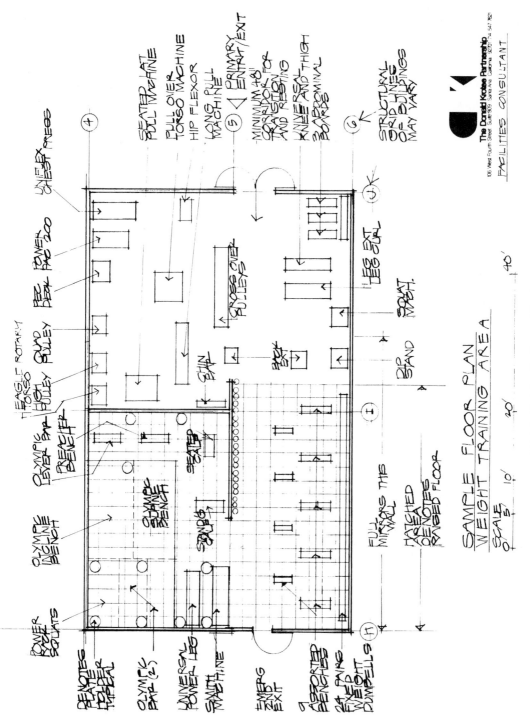

Weight Training Facility and Design

58

Weight Training Resources

This list is prepared to meet the immediate resource needs of consulting, construction, and technical advice concerning the domain of weight training and physical fitness. The names and accompanying addresses provide you with both national and international experience in regard to facility construction, equipment and programmatic structure and design and in sum the A–Z's of weight training and physical fitness.

1. Clark G. Hatch Physical Fitness Centers
   Hawaii Building
   745 Fort Street
   Honolulu, Hawaii 96813
   (808) 536–7205

2. Frederick C. Hatfield
   Weider Health and Fitness
   21100 Erwin Street
   Woodland Hills, California 91364
   (213) 884–6800

3. Donald E. Krotee, AIA
   Architecture and Design
   106 West Fourth Street
   Suite 309
   Santa Ana, California 92701
   (714) 547–7621

4. March L. Krotee
   Division of Physical Education
   University of Minnesota
   218 Cooke Hall
   1900 University Avenue S.E.
   Minneapolis, Minnesota 55455
   (612) 373–4253

5. National Strength and Conditioning Association
   P.O. Box 81410
   Lincoln, Nebraska 68501
   (402) 472–3000

Systems of Training

Contents: *Light to Heavy System*
Heavy to Light System
Rest-pause System
Compound Exercise System
Set System
Cheating System
Split Routine System
Peripheral Heart Action System
Circuit Training System
Super Circuit System
    Nine Station Super Circuit System
Interval Training
Functional Isometrics
Isokinetic Training
Negative Resistance Training
Cyclic Training Systems (Periodization)

Table: *4.1. Model Circuit Training Schedule*
4.2. Example of Yearly Cycle
4.3. Recommended Initial Weight Training Class Schedule
4.4. Weight Training Activities for Sport Specific Purposes
4.5. Selected Exercises and Their Associated Muscle Groups

4

In the preceding chapters, the methods of achieving muscular development and the mechanisms underlying it were discussed. Let us now consider some of the more popular *systems* of training, both those of the past as well as those currently in use. In some cases, aspects of a system may not seem to coincide with physiological principles. It may have been that, in such cases, research efforts of exercise scientists had not been available to the practitioner. In any event, such problems will be pointed out whenever possible. Bear in mind, however, that most systems have become popular because they work! Also, while many of the systems may overlap with regard to underlying principles, often it is the system's unique qualities that have rendered it useful.

A common mistake made by weight trainers, particularly physique artists, is to assume that if an exercise or system works for a champion, then it must be the best system for me. While this is certainly a possibility, it is more probable that it works for champions only because of their greater ability or higher level of fitness. The same system may be too strenuous or too advanced with regard to the finer developmental characteristics for the beginner or intermediate level lifter.

Another common mistake made by many weight trainers is to adopt a system and apply it to all aspects of their regimen, often indiscriminately. While most systems are adaptable to an entire training regimen, there often appear to be problems, such as sticking points, staleness, or overtraining, which necessitate mixing systems. One system may work best for arm development, while another may be more suited to leg or trunk development. Only trial and error over a considerable time period will resolve this problem—indeed, many lifters wallow in despair over such problems for an entire career! The truly open-minded lifters, and the lifters willing to experiment with systems are those who eventually stand a better chance of hitting upon the best combination of systems, and thereby stand a better chance of making rapid progress toward personal goals. One point remains of critical importance; that is, regardless of which system or combination of systems one chooses, strict adherence to basic principles of weight training will yield the best results.

Yet another mistake made by the novice lifter and experienced lifter alike is the practice of keeping few or no training records. It is often asking too much for lifters to look back on their training, and remember which system, how much weight, how many reps and sets, and what the training circumstances surrounding their progress were. Only complete and accurate records can allow a lifter to engage in such reflection, and only such reflection will allow lifters to alter or modify their training regimen according to his or her specific capabilities. The final chapter of this text is devoted to maintenance of accurate training records. The wise and devoted student will do well to heed the example of the great lifters of the past and present, all of whom rely heavily upon such record keeping in establishing training regimen for themselves.

Before progressing into discussion of the various systems of weight training, it should be clear to the student who has read the preceding chapters that any system of training can be adapted to yield maximal gains in any one of the three basic areas—strength or power, hypertrophy, and local muscular endurance. This is so, since it is the *method* of performing each set that largely determines an exercise's function in this regard. Bear in mind, then, throughout the following discussions, that while a particular system may be suited to development of hypertrophy, for example, the basic principles of hypertrophy training must be adhered to in implementing that system in order that the lifter will experience maximal adaptation effects.

Light to Heavy System

This training system achieved popularity among Olympic lifters during the 1930s and 1940s, and consists of progressively adding weight to a bar such that the lifter is able to perform only one repetition. The lifter begins by performing a set of three to five repetitions with a light weight, adds five pounds, performs three to five reps, adds again, and so on until failure. This procedure is followed for each of the lifter's exercises; complete recovery should follow each exercise. For this system to work effectively, three lifters should work together, and a large amount of small weights are required. This system is commonly referred to as pyramiding and may be modified according to the lifters 1-RM%, number of repetitions per set and of course, mode of lifter's activity.

Heavy to Light System

Popularized in the early 1950s, again by Olympic weight lifters, this system is the mirror image of the light to heavy system. The lifter begins each exercise with maximum poundage, performs the given number of reps, removes five pounds, performs more reps, and so on until only the empty bar remains. Fatigue appears to be the key element in this system, as the lifter's capacity to perform the exercise diminishes with each repetition. A variation of this system is to perform each set such that the weight is reduced following each repetition. Again, three lifters are essential, as are large number of small weights.

Rest-pause System

Also called the California Set System, this system involves the lifter performing one repetition with maximal weight, resting a few seconds, performing another repetition, resting, and so on until failure. This system appears to be useful in improving strength, particularly in the learning factor.

Compound Exercise System

In this system, the critical factor is the time element. If the lifter is pressed for time to exercise, two or more individual exercises can be combined to save time. For example, rather than doing curls and presses separately, the lifter curls the weight and presses it in one motion. This system violates the important principle of isolation, since generally only the weaker movement (i.e., in this case, the curl) will benefit from overload.

Set System

By far the most popular and versatile system of weight training, the set system involves performing an exercise for a given number of repetitions, resting a minute or two, repeating, and so on for the required number of sets. This system is adaptable to practically any objective, since the sets and reps can be altered accordingly, as can the resistance, speed, rest period, or cadence. There are many variations of the set system, including the popular *super set system* and the *super multiple set system*. The super set system involves performing an exercise for one set, and following it with one set of an exercise designed to develop the antagonistic muscle(s). For example, curls followed by tricep extensions are together referred to as one super set. The super multiple set system is similar, except that the required number of sets are performed in one exercise before progressing on to the antagonist's exercise, as opposed to alternating them.

Cheating System

In the so-called cheating system, the lifter swings the weight past the weak portion of the movement, and finishes the movement in a strict fashion. This practice enables one to effectively overload the stronger portion of the movement, an area missed by exercising conventionally. For example, the curl movement, due to leverage disadvantage, is weakest near the extended position, and becomes stronger as the elbow nears 90° flexion. By using other muscles synergistically to swing the weight past the extended, weak position, far more weight can be handled in order to overload the stronger, 90°–140° area of movement. When used in conjunction with strict movements, this system is extremely effective in producing total muscular development.

Split Routine System

Generally, this system is employed by body builders who are engaged in developing as many muscles as possible. Since so many exercises are required to achieve total muscular development, lifters split their routines into two groups, and train each group on alternate days. Typically, such grouping might include the following breakdown: Group One (Monday, Wednesday, and Friday), arms, legs, and trunk; Group Two (Tuesday, Thursday, and Saturday), chest, shoulders, and back. The important point in this type of system is to spread the exercises out such that the same muscles are not exercised every day. A common variation of the split routine system is called the *blitz system,* where the lifters perform all their arm exercises on one day, chest exercises the next, legs the next, and so on for the week. This system is generally used by body builders in preparation for a physique competition, and is often used in conjunction or combination with a split routine or some variation of the set system, in order to force as much size increase as possible before the contest. A further variation of the blitz system is the *hourly blitz system,* wherein the lifter blitzes one part of his/her body every hour on the hour all day. Again, this is generally used in the precontest phase, and is not a recommended system for the average athlete due to its extremely strenuous nature.

Peripheral Heart Action System (PHA System)

Blood shunting is the key to this system of training. The lifter performs an exercise, and follows it by an exercise for a muscle or muscle group far removed from the first, then continues on to another exercise far removed from the second, and so on until all of the exercises are performed. The theory is that by keeping the blood in constant circulation, undue fatigue will not be experienced in any given muscle, thereby facilitating recovery and ultimately general muscular development. The exercises are generally arranged in groups, called sequences. The lifter performs all of the exercises of the first sequence, repeats the same sequence three times, moves on to the next sequence, repeats it three times, and so on until five sequences are performed. Each sequence consists of around five exercises for different body parts, and no exercise is repeated in subsequent sequences. There is much to be said for this system of training, especially if one's objective is overall fitness. It is an extremely tiring system, although the fatigue is not of the local variety, but rather of the general, systemic variety. One's heart rate is generally maintained at above 140–150 BPM throughout the exercise session, which normally lasts for an hour or more. Of course the beginning lifter will have to work progressively toward this temporal goal.

Circuit Training System

In many ways related to the PHA system, this system emphasizes the time factor. A circuit consists of a group of exercises, each located at a "station." The lifter attempts to perform all of the exercises within a given "target time," gradually reducing the target time as he or she becomes more fit. For athletes engaged in a specific activity, the exercises included in the circuit should be selected according to the requirements of that activity. An infinite variety of circuits is possible, but should be constructed with basic principles in mind. Generally, this system, like the PHA system, is performed with lighter loads, and is therefore more suited to endurance

Table 4.1. A model circuit training schedule keeping in mind the basic guidelines of warm-up, moderate progressive resistance, alternating muscle groups, and cooling down period.

Circuit Training Schedule	
Duration (Minutes:Seconds)	*Physical Activity*
5:00–7:00 Warm-up	Warm-up consisting of exercise cycling or running in place
30:00–45:00 Exercise Duration	Bench Press or Chest Press Leg Press E-Z Curls Leg Squats Sit-ups with Weight Upright Rows or Dips Hip Flexors or Hanging L's
5:00–10:00 Cooling Down	Cooling down period consisting of static stretching, light calisthenics, and relaxation

development. In fact, there is much evidence to support the notion that these systems are well-suited to the development of cardiovascular/cardiorespiratory functioning. As noted in a previous chapter, however, these claims are open to question in light of the possible inhibitory effects these systems have on the heart's stroke volume, and certainly more research is needed to resolve this issue. A model circuit training schedule may be found in Table 4.1.

Super Circuit System

This system is constructed in similar fashion to the PHA, Set and Circuit Training systems; however, between each station, exercise, or sequence, thirty to forty-five second aerobic exercise such as aerobic dance, cycling, nordic ski machine, running in place, or jumping rope is inserted. This schedule is recommended for the high intensity aerobic general physical activity enthusiast and is another method to insure that the target heart rate is maintained throughout the scheduled exercise period.

An example of a functional nine station Super Circuit Training System complete with specific exercise descriptions and muscle group involvement follows. Further information concerning selected exercises and their associated muscle groups which may be substituted in most exercise schedules may be found in Table 4.5.

Nine Station Super Circuit System

The Super Circuit Training System may be performed in several different variations. For instance, the lifter may perform as many repetitions as possible (using correct form) in a thirty second time interval. This is not usually practical unless the lifter has a partner or trainer to keep track of time. Another more practical method is to perform a given number of repetitions at each station (typically ten to fifteen), selecting a resistance that will be appropriate (35%–55% of 1-RM). Each circuit may be followed by a fifteen second rest period (2:1 work/rest ratio) or more, depending on the lifters level of fitness. It is suggested that the lifter alternate muscle groups to prevent unnecessary localized fatigue. This can be accomplished by alternating upper body and lower body exercises or upper body and midsection exercises. This type of regimen, using light weights, relatively high repetitions, and alternating muscle groups, will enable the lifter to approach and maintain his or her desired target heart rate (140–150 BPM) during the exercise period.

This type of circuit system may be further augmented by the addition of a thirty to sixty second period between each resistance exercise in which the lifter performs some type of typically aerobic activity such as:

1. jumping jacks
2. running in place
3. skipping rope
4. stationary bicycle
5. rowing or nordic ski machine
6. bench stepping
7. aerobic dance

This type of system engaged in three times per week for a ten week period has been shown to produce a significant decrease in lean body mass, and increases in flexed biceps girth, treadmill endurance time, flexibility, strength as well as $Max\dot{V}O_2$ in women. It is also a good calorie burner, resulting in an average of approximately 11 Kcal per minute.

The nine station super circuit system is recommended for apparently healthy individuals with no history of back, knee, or shoulder problems. Exercises should be performed in the order given, preceeded by a five to ten minute warm-up and cool-down period as described in the previous chapter. The lifter should complete the circuit, take a two minute rest and begin again for two to three complete circuits.

1. *Machine Bench Press:* Pectoralis Major, Anterior Deltoid, Triceps
   a. Select the proper weight before beginning the exercise.
   b. Position yourself so that the handles of the machine are directly above the lower fibers of the pectorals (5th rib area).
   c. Grasp the handles at a width which results in your forearms being vertical (neither angling inward nor outward).
   d. Begin by extending the arms upward raising the handles to complete extension of the arms, while exhaling.
   e. Return the weight stack (and handles) to the starting position, gently allowing the weights lifted to touch the rest of the stack; then repeat the movement.
   f. It is best to select a machine which provides a separate weight stack and handle for each arm so as to provide uniform resistance to each side of the body.
2. *Half Squats Using a Squat Machine:* Gluteus Maximus, Hamstrings, Quadriceps, Erector Spinae Group
   a. Position feet flat on the floor directly beneath the shoulder pads of the squat machine with the heels 16 to 18 inches apart and toes pointing outward at a 20° angle. A vertical squat machine with a shoulder attachment that is adjustable to varying heights is recommended. There are only a couple on the market at present. A machine is preferable

to a barbell in a circuit program because of the quickness and ease of weight selection and because a machine can be used with relative safety and without the need of spotters.

  b. Adjust the height of the shoulder pads so that the upper and lower leg form an 80° angle when feet are positioned as described and the shoulders are pressed slightly into the shoulder pads. This is the starting position for the exercise, with back flat, feet flat on the floor, and hips 6 to 8 inches behind the shoulders.

  c. From this position tighten the back, hips, and legs, then begin to extend the hips and legs until reaching an upright position, but do not lock or hyperextend the knees.

  d. Return to the start position, lightly touching the plates to the remainder of the weight stack, and return to an upright posture.

  e. Exhale during the extension or upward portion of the exercise, and inhale on the way down (during the eccentric phase).

  f. Remember to keep the back tight and flat at all times, and keep the head up.

3. *Machine Biceps Curls:* Biceps, Brachii, Brachialis

  a. Select the proper weight to be lifted.

  b. Position the upper arms on the arm pad and grasp the bar with a supinated (palms up) grip.

  c. Being sure that the entire surface of the backs of the arms remains in contact with the pad, flex the arms, lifting the bar to chin level.

  d. Allow arms to extend and return the weight to the starting position, then repeat.

4. *Clean and Press:* Erector Spinae Group, Gluteals, Quadriceps, Hamstrings, Trapezius, Deltoids, Triceps, Serratus Anterior

  a. This is really two separate exercises combined into one very comprehensive total body lift.

  b. To enable a lifter to incorporate this exercise into a circuit program, a complete set of fixed weight barbells is necessary. This provides easy and quick weight selection.

  c. Address the bar with feet twelve to fourteen inches apart, toes straight ahead, and shins within two inches of touching the bar.

  d. Reach down and grasp the bar firmly (palms down) with a shoulder width grip. At the same time assume a position with hips below shoulder, back flat, head up, arms straight, and feet flat.

  e. Tighten all muscles of back, hip, legs, and shoulders prior to beginning the exercise.

  f. Extend the hips, back, and legs, forcefully lifting the bar off the floor vertically. During the lift the hips should never raise up faster or sooner than the shoulders. In other words, the angle of the torso to the legs should never decrease, only increase. This assures that you are using leg and hip strength to start the bar moving.

  g. As the body reaches to an erect position, the bar is kept close to the body and the arms which have remained straight, up to this point, begin to flex; the shoulders are shrugged using the trapezius muscles, and the lifter raises up on the toes.

  h. The arms, shoulders, and trapezius muscles maintain the momentum imparted to the bar by the legs, hips, and back; the bar is lifted vertically and the elbows snapped below the bar, and the bar is "caught" momentarily on the anterior deltoids.

     i. From this position stand erect, and extend the arms pressing the bar vertically overhead until arms are fully extended.

     j. Return the bar first to the shoulders, then to the floor, and repeat the entire movement.

5. *Calf Raises:* Gastrocnemius, Soleus, Peroneus Longus and Brevis, Tibialis Posterior, Flexor Digitorum Longus

    a. Position the balls of the feet over the rear edge of the toe board of the calf machine, and place shoulders into the shoulder pads.

    b. Extend the legs and lift the weight stack to an erect position with knees locked.

    c. Lower the heels below the toe board to pre-stretch the calf muscles. Then extend the foot and raise the heel as high as possible maintaining straight knees.

    d. Return the heels to the starting position and repeat movement.

6. *Dips:* Triceps, Anterior Deltoids, Pectoralis Major and Minor, Latissimus Dorsi, Teres Major

    a. Begin by supporting yourself on your hands with arms locked and body hanging vertically on dipping apparatus.

    b. Lower body slowly until the upper arm is approximately parallel or below parallel with the floor. (The arm will be flexed.)

    c. Extend the arms and return the body back to the starting position. Repeat.

    d. A good dipping apparatus should be high enough so that the user's feet cannot touch the floor in the low position. It should also include feet pedestals so that the lifter is not required to jump into position.

    e. This exercise can also be performed with additional weight. This requires the use of a special belt and chain from which weights can be suspended while performing the exercise.

7. *Back Extensions:* Erector Spinae Group, Hamstrings, Gluteus Maximus, Trapezius, Rhomboids

    a. Position yourself on the back extension apparatus in a prone position, achilles tendons under the leg pads, navel approximately four inches in front of the leading edge of the padded surface.

    b. If you plan to use extra weight, we suggest an Olympic plate held behind the head. If you do not intend to use extra weight clasp the hands behind the head.

    c. Lower your head and shoulders until your torso forms a 90° angle with your legs. At this point raise the head and shoulders so that the back is straight and parallel to the floor.

    d. Keep elbows back as you raise the torso, and look up with the head as the torso reaches parallel. This will exercise the trapezius and rhomboid muscles as well as the spinal erectors.

    e. Return to the starting position (torso flexed) and repeat.

8. *Incline Bent Knee Sit-ups:* Rectus Abdominis, Iiacus, Psoas Major and Minor, Pectineus, Rectus Femoris

    a. Position the knee sit-up board at an incline that will permit only twenty to twenty-five sit-ups with good form. This may require some trial and error.

    b. Secure the feet with knees bent at 90°, back and head resting on the board, hands alongside the head or in front of the head (not clasped behind the head).

    c. Begin by tucking chin to the chest and flexing the spine forward one vertebra at a time as if you are rolling up a carpet.

    d. Continue forward flexion raising the lower back off the board and bringing shoulders within six inches of the knees, exhaling during this phase.

    e. Return the back and head to the board by reversing the flexion movements as if you are unrolling a carpet. Be sure you return the head to the board as well as the shoulders, in order to achieve the maximum stretch for the rectus abdominis muscles. Inhale during this phase.

    f. Repeat the movement.

9. *Lat Pulldowns:* Latissimus Dorsi, Teres Major, Rhomboids, Biceps

    a. Sit on a stool or bench or kneel on the floor below the high pulley station.

    b. Position your shoulders either directly under the bar or slightly in front of it.

    c. Take a wide grip on the bar (slightly more than shoulder width) and begin with arms straight.

    d. Flex arms and rotate scapulae so as to pull the bar down behind the neck touching the bar gently on or about the seventh cervical vertebra.

    e. Slowly allow the bar to raise so that the arms are once again extended overhead in the starting position.

    f. Repeat.

Interval Training

While interval training techniques have traditionally been used for endurance events in athletics, they may be adaptable to weight training as well. In interval training, short bursts of activity are alternated with periods of rest for recovery. The duration and intensity of the activity and rest periods are closely monitored, and successively shorter rest periods, together with successively longer, more intense activity periods is the objective. The principle of progressive overload is served in one of five ways: (1) progressively increasing the duration of the activity interval, (2) increasing the intensity of the activity interval, (3) decreasing the duration of the recovery interval, (4) increasing the intensity of the activity during recovery (complete rest is not advised, since some muscular activity is required for removal of lactic acid and other metabolites), and (5) increasing the repetition of the interval. Generally, one's heart rate is kept at a minimum of 150 BPM during the activity interval, and maintained at around 110–120 BPM during the recovery interval.

A wide variety of intervals have been devised for endurance athletes. In weight training, light weights are generally used in a fashion similar to the PHA system and circuit training techniques mentioned above.

Functional Isometrics

Functional isometrics combines, to a limited extent, qualities of both isotonic contraction (an actual shortening of the muscle takes place) and isometric contraction (static contracture against an immovable object). Initially, the lifter explosively moves the weight two to four inches against retaining pins, and sustains exertion against the pins in an isometric fashion for about five seconds. Theoretically, the initial isotonic phase of the exercise forces neuromuscular adaptation insofar as the movement pattern is concerned, while the isometric phase is largely concerned with intensity of effort in forcing adaptation. The harder one tries to push against the retaining pins, the more motor units are forced into action.

One of the drawbacks of purely isometric training is that one becomes stronger only at the angle at which the muscle is being exercised, a phenomenon presumed to be resultant of neuromuscular function. A drawback of isotonic training is that only the weakest portion of a movement can be overloaded effectively. Functional isometrics appears to be a method of reducing these drawbacks, in that only a limited range of movement is used (typically, the weakest part of a movement, called the sticking point), thereby facilitating overload without attendant neuromuscular specialization to the point where only that location in the movement is strengthened. Research is scanty at best, particularly in regard to the psychological and physiological mechanisms underlying this system's usefulness. However, if one can trust the experience of the great lifters of our time, many of whom use this system adjunctively with other systems, moderate to exceptional improvement in strength can be achieved. Because of the high intensity of effort involved in this system, it is recommended as a preseason system, to be employed for no more than a four to six week period. For competitive weight lifters, it is suited for precontest peaking, but not especially recommended for off-season training except for possible remedial purposes.

Isokinetic Training

Isokinetic training appears to effectively circumvent virtually all of the drawbacks of conventional systems of training. In fact, most of the research reviewed indicates that this system at least has the potential to equal or exceed (in some cases by a considerable margin) the development capabilities offered by isometrics or isotonics. Basically, this system employs a method of accommodating resistance—that is, the speed of movement is held constant, thereby allowing for complete overload throughout the entire range of a muscle's movement. Specialized apparatuses engineered to accomplish this speed control are used and, while generally rather expensive, are extremely adaptable to meet individual exercise requirements. One manufacturer's description of isokinetic exercise, corroborated by numerous research reports, reads as follows:

> Resistance is a function of the force applied. The isokinetic device retards the speed at which the user can move throughout a "full range of motion." The load will accommodate anything from fingertip pressure to hundreds of pounds. The user applies maximum effort and an isokinetic device automatically varies the resistance. As the muscle's tension capacity and skeletal advantage varies through the range of movement, the resistance naturally accommodates to the muscle's force transmitting capacity at every point in the range. Isokinetic constantly loads the muscles near their maximum with each repetition regardless if it is the second or tenth repetition of the exercise, and without overstressing or understressing the muscles at any point. Thus, the accommodating resistance of the exerciser correlates to the user's immediate and specific muscular capacity.

There are tremendous advantages to such a system, to be sure. Probably the best advice at this time would be to supplement other weight-training systems with isokinetic training. Specific movement patterns related to individual sports may often be difficult to perform on such devices, therefore making it necessary to include exercises which facilitate skilled movements as well. This would be especially true for Olympic weight lifters involved in moving the bar in specific patterns, often requiring ballistic muscular action and generation of stretch reflex, functions not capable of being reproduced isokinetically. Nonetheless, isokinetic training appears to offer one of the best alternatives to weight training devised. It will be interesting to observe this system's progress over the next few years, as well as the many records which promise to be broken as a direct result of isokinetically developed performance capacity.

Although background research involving methods and systems of training isokinetically is minimal, what has been accomplished indicates that the same basic considerations with regard to repetitions, sets, resistance and cadence should be adhered to as in conventional training systems. As in other systems, the SAID, overload and isolation principles apply in isokinetics.

Negative Resistance Training

As discussed previously, isotonic contractions are of two general categories—concentric and eccentric. While concentric contractions involve a shortening of the gross muscle, as in flexing the elbow, eccentric contractions is that phase of the movement wherein the muscle is lengthened against resistance, as in lowering the weight after curling it. Research indicates that eccentric (or negative) movements are only about one-third as costly, from the standpoint of energy expenditure, as concentric contractions. Since gravity is acting upon the weight being lifted in a constant amount, more muscular exertion must be used to raise the weight than to lower it. In other words, more motor units are responding in the concentric portion of the exercise than in the eccentric portion. However, if one were to use excessively large weights and perform the eccentric portion of the lift with a partner or partners assisting in returning the weight to the starting point between each repetition, far greater numbers of motor units appear to be stimulated to respond. There is some evidence that such a system of training can yield greater strength than its concentric counterpart which uses far lighter weights. Apparently the concentric portion of a lift suffers the disadvantage of being effective only at the weakest angle of the movement, whereas the lowered weight, by controlling the speed of descent, suffers no such disadvantage. It may, however, cause severe discomfort because of the myofibrillar elements being damaged. The raking of the tiny cross-bridges across one another seems to produce friction in excessive amounts, as well as tearing of the individual elements, causing muscular soreness which may last for several days.

The advantages offered by the negative movements are, from most reports, outweighed by the inherent disadvantages—the soreness and the difficulty involved in finding lifters capable of effectively acting as partners. Further, in light of the recently developed isokinetic theory, which overloads the entire range of movement in a concentric fashion while at the same time completely eliminating the eccentric portion, negative training appears to be of limited merit. Many physique artists, wishing to garner as much size increase as possible from their regimen, still use negative training, but generally do so with the same amount of weight as they use in the concentric phase of the exercise—in fact, they perform them together. This practice is referred to as *continuous tension* exercising, and involves lifting the weight through only a portion of the total movement without resting between repetitions. Also called *partials,* or *burns,* this system emphasizes overloading individual segments of an exercise differentially, according to which muscle is being isolated, and/or which portion of the joint action is stronger or weaker from a leverage perspective. There is much to be said for this practice, as it apparently has been very effective in yielding great gains in muscular size.

Cyclic Training Systems (Periodization)

All athletes need to be aware of how to get the most out of their yearly training in order to maximize their competitive efforts. However, many athletes all too often peak for a contest or meet too early in the season, and consequently are "burned out" by the time the season's end approaches. They forget that the most important meets of the season are generally at the end of the season. Consequently, a cyclic system, which necessarily differs for each sport (in fact, very possibly for each athlete) must be devised which will allow athletes to achieve their optimal potential at the important meets rather than at the earlier less important ones. The principles governing cyclic training are similar for all sports, although the specific methods and systems followed may vary considerably. Generally, all athletes should divide their year into four phases: developmental, preparation, competition, and recovery. A brief description of cyclic training was presented in Chapter 2.

During the *developmental period,* Phase I which lasts about four months, the athlete concentrates on skills that he or she has had difficulty with during the previous competitive season. Specific physical requirements are maximized during this period. For competitive weight lifters, it is power, while for long-distance runners it is endurance, including cardiovascular/respiratory endurance as well as local muscular endurance. During the *preparation phase,* Phase II athletes should hone their skills to a fine edge, increasing the intensity of the workouts. This phase lasts for about three months, and precedes the actual competition phase. During the *competition phase,* Phase III the athlete maintains very high intensity in all workouts, and works those skills and physical attributes which he or she has found to be deficient after the first two or three meets. For most sports, the competition season lasts for about four months. It is, therefore, imperative that the athlete identify beforehand those meets or contests which are of greatest importance and attempt to peak for those. This is accomplished in the following manner. Choose the two most important meets, and train for them, regarding all other meets as practice sessions. For the less-important meets, do not cut back on workout intensity the week prior to the meet, but do so for the important ones in order that complete recovery is effected. Also, do not discontinue supportive exercises before less important meets, but do so for important ones.

While specific requirements may vary for individuals or sports, Table 4.2, devised by a leading weight lifting expert, is illustrative of the general concept of cyclic training. The table presented is meant to be a guide for beginning Olympic weight lifters.

Table 4.2. Example of a Yearly Cycle

	Phase I	Phase II	Phase III	Phase IV
Technique	60%	40%	30%	30%
Power	20%	40%	10%	10%
Olympic Lifts	10%	15%	60%	20%
Fitness	10%	5%	0%	40%

As can be observed in the above table, the *recovery phase,* Phase IV emphasizes total fitness and technique. In the case of the Olympic weight lifter, this fitness emphasis would relate to endurance work, while for another athlete, power might be emphasized. The principle is that one should work on overall fitness while recovering, and particularly those aspects of fitness in which he or she is generally deficient.

There appears to be little use for cyclic training in body building. The current trend among physique artists is to stay in peak condition the year round, varying workouts and diet only a few weeks before each competition. It's very difficult to put on muscle mass, so most physique artists tend to keep what they have—in fact, increase it—all year. Higher reps with lighter weights are used just prior to contest time, and diet is rigidly controlled to drop as much body fat and water weight as possible. This is to expose the muscle to its greatest advantage, without excess water or fat filling the striations of the peripheral musculature. This procedure is referred to as "cutting up" and is definitely not a recommended practice for the average lifter, athlete, or general physical activity enthusiast. In fact, most physique artists admit to fatigue and lethargy after such a cutting up period. There are many misconceptions concerning athlete's diets, and these will be covered in a later chapter. For now, however, it should be fairly obvious that such a contest diet violates practically all of the principles of sound nutrition, and the physique artist would be the first to admit it. That is why it is employed only before selected contests and for a two-week period at the most.

While physical activity should play an integral part in everyone's life style, weight training should definitely play a part in everyone's personalized training regimen as well as in sport related activity. Tables 4.3 and 4.4 illustrate examples of an initial weight training classes' guide to progressive resistance training as well as various generalized recommended strength training activities for sport specific activity. For the systems approach to training to be effective it should be individualized keeping in mind the aims and objectives of the participant and the participant's level of fitness, age, sex, sport specific designated position, as well as various psychosocial parameters.

Table 4.3. Initial phases of a beginning general weight training class program which must be further adapted to meet individual goals concerning the development of muscular endurance, hypertrophy, and explosive strength.

Recommended Initial Weight Training Class Schedule

Variables Cyclic Phase Level of Fitness Activity Intensity	*Initial Fitness* **Beginning** Light/Moderate	*Skill (Technique)* **Intermediate** Medium/High	*Elevated Intensity Levels* **Advanced** High/Heavy
Frequency/Week	3	3–4	3–6
Duration: Minutes/Workout	30–45	45–90	45–130
Workouts/Day	1–2	2–3	3–5
Number of Selected Exercises	8–16	8–12	8–12
Technique Concentration	3 days/week	3 days/week	1–2 days/week
Intensity Level/1-RM%	20–60%	50–85%	70–100%
Number of Repetitions	5–15	3–6	1–8
Number of Sets	2–4	2–5	3–5
Mode of Activity	Sets, repetitions, and various individualized system approaches presented in this chapter.		
Warm-up/Cool Down:Minutes/Workout	10–15	7–12	7–10
Training Cycle:Weeks (10–16 week class periods at 3 meetings per week)	4–8	4–10	2–8

Table 4.4. Weight training activities for sport specific purpose. J. P. O'Shea, *Scientific Principles and Methods of Strength Fitness,* © 1976, Addison-Wesley, Reading, Massachusetts, pp. 92–93. Reprinted by permission.

Sport Specific Activity or Event

Mode of Activity	Badminton	Baseball	Basketball	Cycling	Football	Golf	Gymnastics	Ice Hockey	Nordic (cross country) skiing	Racquetball	Rowing	Skiing (downhill)	Soccer	Backstroke	Breaststroke	Butterfly	Freestyle	Tennis	Sprinting	Hurdling	Javelin	Long Jump	Distance Running	Pole Vault	High Jump	Discus and Shot Put	Volleyball	Wrestling
														Swimming					Track and Field									
Neck flexion and extension		X	X				X						X															X
Shoulder shrug		X	X					X	X				X	X				X	X			X			X		X	
Military or overhead press		X		X			X	X					X			X	X		X							X	X	X
Behind the neck press														X	X												X	
Upright rowing	X	X	X	X			X	X	X	X	X	X	X	X	X	X	X							X	X			
Bent rowing		X	X										X				X		X								X	X
Lat machine	X		X	X			X	X	X	X	X	X	X	X	X	X			X									X
Triceps extension		X					X	X	X				X			X	X	X	X			X	X	X		X	X	X
Lateral arm raise		X					X		X				X	X					X						X		X	
Bent-arm pull-over		X	X						X		X		X	X	X	X						X	X	X	X		X	
Biceps curl							X						X														X	
Dumbbell curl	X		X		X	X	X			X	X	X	X						X	X		X	X	X				X
Bench press		X	X										X		X	X	X		X					X	X	X	X	X
Incline press		X					X	X	X					X	X	X			X			X	X	X	X	X		
Parallel bar dip							X	X	X	X	X	X					X											X
Back hyperextension	X						X		X				X		X		X		X						X		X	X
Trunk extension		X						X		X	X								X							X	X	X
Weighted sit-ups	X	X	X	X	X	X		X	X	X	X	X	X					X	X			X	X	X	X	X	X	X
Hip flexion	X		X					X		X				X	X	X	X						X					
Stiff leg dead lift		X	X	X					X			X			X	X							X					X
Knee flexion		X							X								X	X	X	X	X							X
Knee extension		X	X	X				X	X			X	X	X					X	X	X	X		X	X		X	X
Squat	X	X	X	X	X	X			X			X	X											X			X	X
Hack squat		X			X	X	X	X	X	X	X			X	X	X	X	X	X	X	X	X	X	X	X	X	X	
Toe raise	X	X	X						X	X		X							X	X	X			X	X	X		X
Waist	X	X	X	X			X	X		X	X		X						X						X	X		X

Included in all systems of training should be the systematic and selective exercise of the various muscle groups. Table 4.5 presents some of the more common muscles and muscle groups and describes the systematic employment of free weights, Universal Gym and Nautilus equipment.

Table 4.5. Selected exercises and their associated muscle groups. Adapted from J. A. Peterson, *Total Fitness: The Nautilus Way*. Leisure Press, West Point, New York, 1978. Used by permission.

Muscle Group	Barbells/Dumbbells	Universal Gym	Nautilus Machines
Gluteus maximus/lower back (proceed with caution)	half squat stiff-legged deadlift good mornings squat	squat leg press hyperextension	hip and back squat leg press
Quadriceps	squat hack squat half squat	leg extension leg press leg squat real runner	leg extension and super leg extension squat leg press
Hamstrings	squat half squat	leg curl leg press	leg curl squat leg press compound leg hip duo and back
Gastrocnemius	toe raise calf raise	toe press on leg press	calf raise on multi exercise toe press on leg press

Latissimus dorsi	bent-over row
	bent-armed pullover
	stiff-armed pullover
	incline press
		chin-up
		pulldown on lat
		  machine
			pullover
			behind neck
			torso/arm
			chin-up on multi
			  exercise

Trapezius	shoulder shrug dumbbell shoulder shrug bent-over row	shoulder shrug	neck and shoulder rowing torso
Waist, hand and forearm	wrist curls Thor's hammer reverse curls	hand gripper wrist conditioner	wrist curl on multi exercise
Foot and ankle	ankle curls toe presses	leg press squat	leg press squat

Deltoids	bench press
	press behind neck
	upright rowing
	forward raise
	side raise with
	  dumbbells
	front raise with
	  dumbbells
		seated press
		upright rowing
			double shoulder
			1. lateral raise
			2. overhead press
			omni shoulder
			rowing torso

Table 4.5—*Continued*

Muscle Group	Barbells/Dumbbells	Universal Gym	Nautilus Machines
Pectoralis majors	bench press dumbbell flies incline press parallel bar dips	bench press parallel dip	double chest 1. arm cross 2. decline press 3. parallel dip on multi exercise
Biceps	standing curl E-Z curl preacher curls upright row	curl chin-up	compound curl bicep curl omni curl
Triceps	tricep extension French press	press down on lat machine	compound tricep tricep extension omni tricep
Abdominals/obliques	bent leg sit-ups side bend with dumbbells	abdominal conditioner sit-up leg raise	sit-up on multi exercise leg raise on multi exercise
Neck (proceed with caution)	side twist with bar head harness bridges neck twists	neck conditioner	4-way neck rotary neck neck and shoulder

Specialized Exercises and Apparatuses

Contents: *Movement Descriptors*

Figures: *Descriptive sequence photographs are presented for each of the exercises covered as well as for the women's daily dozen.*

*Exercises dealing with the neck (cervical and thoracic spine area), trunk (lower back region) such as hyperextensions and good mornings, and the knee such as squatting exercises should be undertaken with caution. Proper warm-up, progressive resistance, lifting techniques, and the use of experienced spotters are recommended.

5

This chapter catalogues many of the most widely used exercises and the apparatuses upon which or with which they are performed. The student should bear in mind that many of the exercises are highly specialized in the sense that they yield specific results. Accordingly, it remains imperative that the student adopt those exercises that suit his or her specific objectives—no athlete should perform all the exercises catalogued here within the same program. The preceding chapters are therefore required reading before delving into an exercise program, for they are designed to give the student insight as to the proper methods of exercising, as well as assisting in clarifying personal objectives.

The catalogue system employed in this chapter involves a basic approach. Each body part (i.e., the major joints) is discussed separately with regard to the movements each is capable of performing. The muscles which are listed are, for clarity, the prime movers—the assistant movers, stabilizers, and synergists are not listed. If the student's training regimen must become so complex as to require consideration of these other muscles, reference to any good kinesiology text is recommended. Listed below is a brief definition of each of the terms used to describe the various movements included in this chapter.

Movement Descriptors

Movements of the Elbow Joint

flexion—drawing the hand toward the shoulder
extension—straightening the arm

Movements of the Forearm (Radio-ulnar Joint)

pronation—turning forearm so thumbs point toward the body (palms down)
supination—turning forearm so thumbs point away from the body (palms up)

Movements of the Shoulder Joint

flexion—raising arm forward from side
extension—lowering arm from flexed position to side

adduction—lowering arm from sideward extension toward body
abduction—raising arm from side laterally
horizontal flexion—drawing arm across body from sideward extension
horizontal extension—moving arm from flexed position to sideward extension
inward rotation—turning arm forward (accompanies forearm pronation)
outward rotation—turning arm backward (accompanies forearm supination)

Movements of the Shoulder Girdle (Scapular Movements)

elevation—drawing shoulders upward as in shrugging
depression—drawing shoulders downward toward sides
abduction—spreading shoulders so as to broaden back
adduction—drawing shoulders together so as to pinch scapulae
upward rotation—scapulae rotate upward accommodating arm elevation above head
downward rotation—arms drawn against side causes scapulae to rotate downward

Movements of the Spinal Column

Cervical Spine (Neck)

flexion—chin to chest
extension—facing straight ahead (spine hyperextended when looking up)
lateral flexion—while looking straight ahead, cocking head left or right
rotation (same side)—rotation of head and shoulders toward muscle's side
rotation (opposite side)—rotation away from side muscle is located on

Thoracic and Lumbar Spine (Midtrunk and Lower Trunk)

flexion—drawing of ribs toward pelvis frontwards
extension—standing erect (bending backward in spinal hyperextension)
lateral flexion—bending sideways left or right
rotation (same side)—rotation of head and shoulders toward muscle's side
rotation (opposite side)—rotation away from side muscle is located on

Movements of the Hip Joint

flexion—drawing knees toward chest
extension—upper leg in line with pelvis and spine as in standing erect
adduction—drawing legs together from side straddle position
abduction—separating legs toward side straddle position
inward rotation—turning leg inward, as in walking pigeon-toed
outward rotation—turning legs outward, as in walking with toes pointing out

Movements of the Knee Joint

flexion—drawing heels toward buttocks
extension—straightening leg as in erect standing position
inward rotation—with knee flexed at 90°, turning toes inward
outward rotation—with knee flexed at 90°, turning toes outward

Movements of the Ankle and Foot

    dorsiflexion—drawing toes toward front of leg
    plantar flexion—pointing toes as in standing on toes
    inversion—soles of feet facing inward (accompanies plantar flexion)
    eversion—soles of feet face outward (accompanies dorsiflexion)

Exercises for the Arms (Elbow and Radio-ulnar Joints)

Flexion. Biceps brachii, brachialis, brachioradialis

Figure 5.1. Alternate dumbbell curls

Figure 5.2. E–Z curls

Figure 5.3. Concentration curls

Figure 5.4. Preacher bench curls

Extension. Triceps brachii

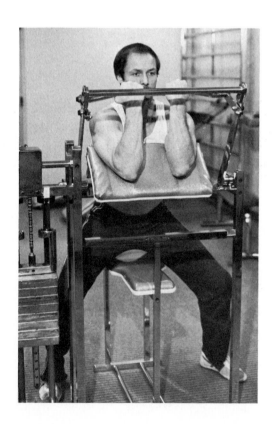

Figure 5.5. Machine curls

Figure 5.6. Tricep extensions

Figure 5.7. Standing tricep extensions

Figure 5.8. French presses

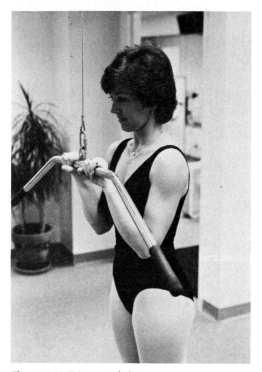
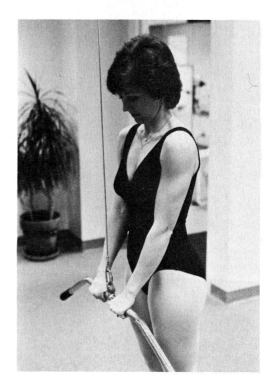

Figure 5.9. Tricep pushdowns

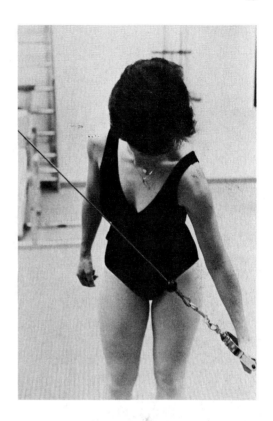

Figure 5.10. Tricep kickbacks

Supination. Supinator

Pronation. Pronator quadratus

Figure 5.11. Thor's hammer

Figure 5.12. Thor's hammer

Exercises for the Muscles of the Shoulder Joint

Flexion. Anterior deltoid, clavicular pectoralis major

Figure 5.13. Front raises

Figure 5.14. Alternate front raises

Figure 5.15. Dips with elbows out

Figure 5.16. Weighted dips

Figure 5.17. Incline presses

Figure 5.18. Incline flys

Figure 5.19. Prone fly

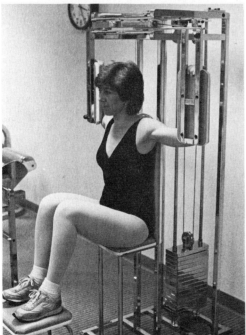

Figure 5.20. Vertical butterfly

Extension. Sternal pectoralis major, latissimus dorsi, teres major

Figure 5.21. Kneeling front pulldowns

Figure 5.22. Seated front pulldowns (reverse grip)

Figure 5.23. Decline presses

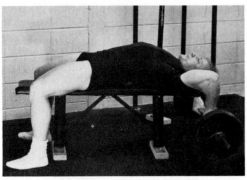

Figure 5.24. Pullovers

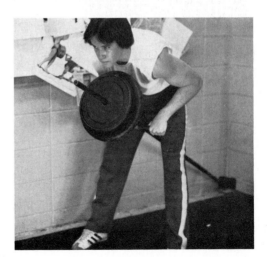

Figure 5.25. Bent rows with elbows in (two methods)

Figure 5.25—*Continued*

Adduction. Sternal pectoralis major, latissimus dorsi, teres major

Figure 5.26. Kneeling pulldowns

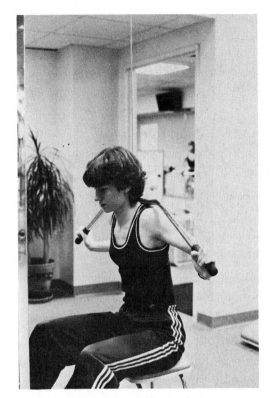

Figure 5.27. Seated pulldowns

Figure 5.28. Wide grip weighted dips

Abduction. Middle deltoid, supraspinatus

Figure 5.29. Lateral raises

Figure 5.30. Upright rows

Horizontal Flexion. Anterior deltoid, sternal, and clavicular pectoralis.

Figure 5.31. Bench press

Figure 5.32. Supine flys

Horizontal Extension. Middle and posterior deltoid, infraspinatus, teres minor

Figure 5.33. Bent rows with wide grip

Inward and Outward Rotation. The muscles involved in these movements (infraspinatus, sub-scapularis, and the teres major and minor) are used either as prime movers or assistant movers in other actions of the shoulder joint. No special exercises for these rotational movements are recommended.

Exercises for Muscles of the Shoulder Girdle (Scapular Movements)

Elevation. Trapezius I and II, levator scapulae, rhomboids

Figure 5.34. Shoulder shrugs

Depression. Subclavius, pectoralis minor, trapezius IV

Figure 5.35. Straight arm dips

Abduction. Pectoralis minor, serratus anterior. As in shoulder joint rotation, these muscles are involved in other movements as well as abduction, and therefore need not be exercised employing pure abduction movements.

Adduction. Trapezius III, rhomboids

Figure 5.36. Seated cable rows

Upward Rotation. Serratus anterior, trapezius III and IV

Figure 5.37. Standing military press

Figure 5.38. Seated military press

Figure 5.39. Seated machine press

Figure 5.40. Alternate seated shoulder press

Figure 5.41. Supine machine bench press

Figure 5.42. Top half lateral raises

Downward Rotation. Pectoralis minor, rhomboids

Figure 5.43. Pulldowns with narrow grip

Exercises for Muscles of the Neck (Cervical Spine)

Flexion. Sternocleidomastoid

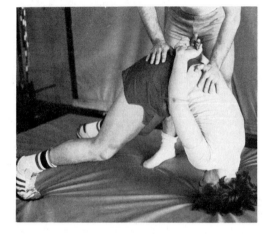

Figure 5.44. Front bridges

Figure 5.45. Head harness

Extension. Splenius group, erector spinae group, semispinalis group, deep posterior spinal group

Figure 5.46. Back bridges

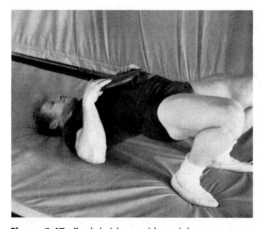

Figure 5.47. Back bridges with weight

Lateral Flexion. Sternocleidomastoid, scaleni group, splenius group, erector spinae group, semispinalis group, intertransversarii, multifidus

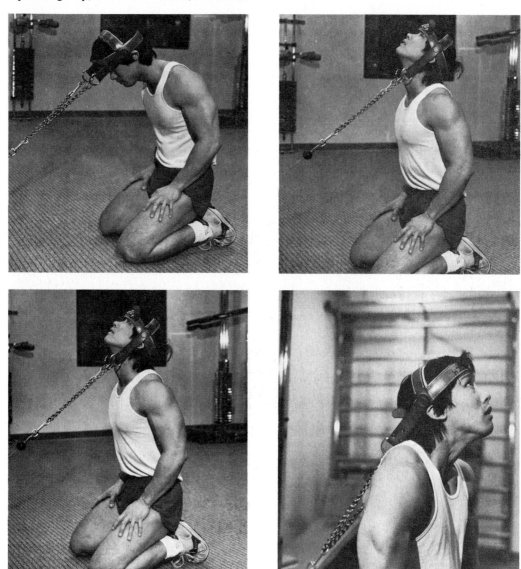

Figure 5.48. Machine head harness

Rotation to Same and Opposite Sides. Splenius group, erector spinae group, semispinalis cervicus, sternocleidomastoid, rotatores, multifidus

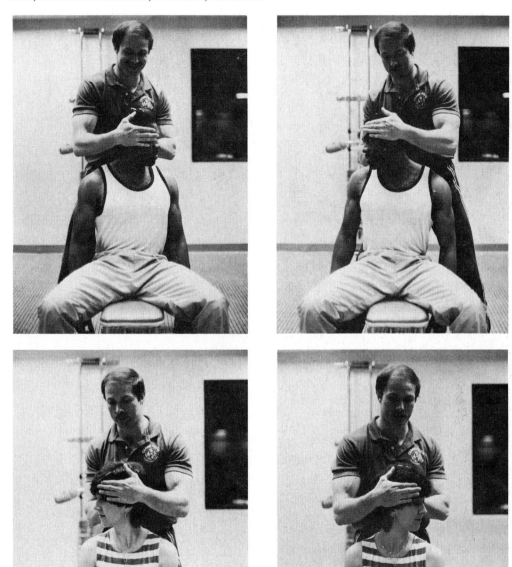

Figure 5.49. Head twists (partner)

Exercises for Muscles of the Trunk (Thoracic and Lumbar Spine)

Flexion. Rectus abdominis, external obliques, internal obliques

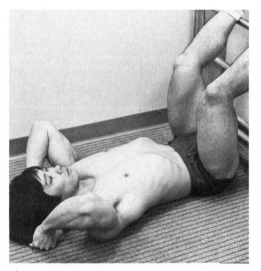

Figure 5.50. Crunchers

Figure 5.51. Leg raises (weighted or unweighted)

Figure 5.51—*Continued*

Figure 5.52. Bent leg sit-ups

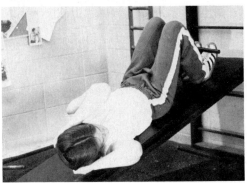
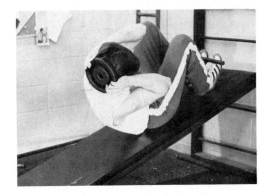

Figure 5.53. Twisted sit-ups

Extension. Erector spinae group, semispinalis thoracis, deep posterior spinal group

Figure 5.54. Hyperextensions

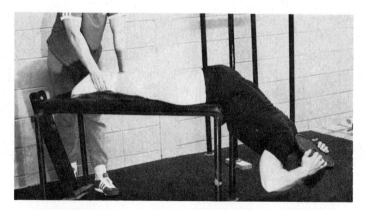

Figure 5.55. Hyperextensions with weight

Figure 5.56. Good mornings

Figure 5.57. Elevated pulls

Lateral Flexion. Internal obliques, external obliques, quadratus lumborum, erector spinae group, intertransversarii, multifidus

Figure 5.58. Barbell side bends

Rotation Same and Opposite Sides. Internal obliques, external obliques, erector spinae group, semispinalis thoracis, rotatores, multifidus

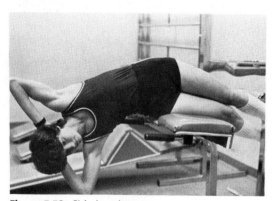 

Figure 5.59. Side bends

Figure 5.60. Machine side bends

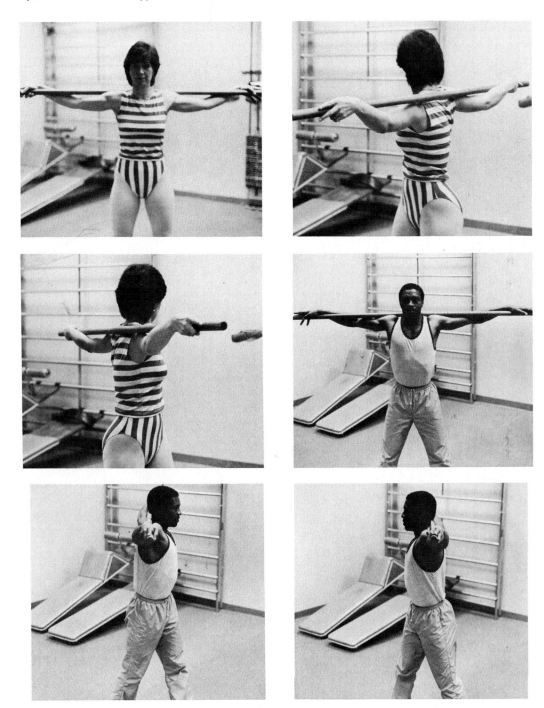

Figure 5.61. Trunk twists

Exercises for Muscles of the Hip Joint (Buttocks and Thighs)

Flexion. Psoas, iliacus, rectus femoris, pectineus

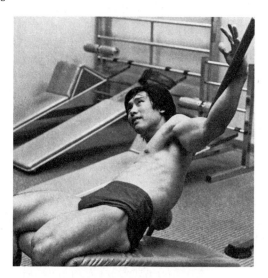

Figure 5.62. Decline trunk twists

Figure 5.63. Leg raises (weighted or unweighted)

 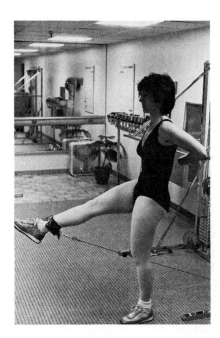

Figure 5.64. Front leg kicks (pulley)

Extension. Gluteus maximus, bicep femoris (long head), semitendinosis, semimembranosis

Figure 5.65. Stiff legged dead lifts
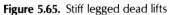

Figure 5.66. Bent legged dead lifts

Figure 5.67. Supine leg kicks (pulley)

Figure 5.68. Full squat

Abduction. Gluteus medius

Figure 5.69. Outward leg kicks (pulley)

Adduction. Pectineus, gracilis, adductor group

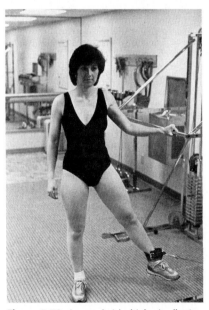

Figure 5.70. Inward side kicks (pulley)

Inward and Outward Rotation. Tensor fasciae latae, gluteus maximus, gluteus minimus, outward rotator group. These muscles are generally strengthened via other exercises, and consequently have no special exercises which are specifically designed for hip rotation.

Exercises for Muscles of the Knee Joint

Flexion. Semimembranosis, semitendinosis, biceps femoris (hamstring group)

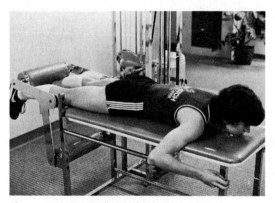 

Figure 5.71. Prone leg curls

Figure 5.72. Standing leg curls

Figure 5.73. Half squat

Figure 5.74. Leg presses

Extension. Rectus femoris, vastus lateralis, vastus medialis, vastus intermedius (quadricep group)

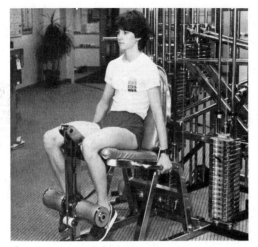

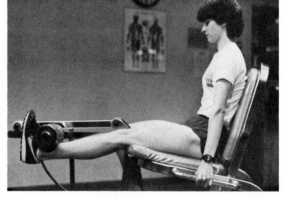

Figure 5.75. Single leg extensions

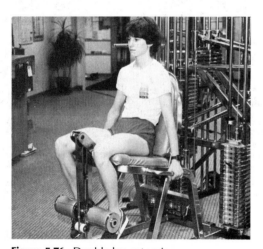

Figure 5.76. Double leg extensions

Figure 5.77. Hack squat

Figure 5.78. Leg presses

Inward and Outward Rotation. Semimembranosis, semitendinosis, popliteus, biceps femoris. These muscles are generally strengthened via other exercises. Therefore, specific exercises are not necessary.

Exercises for Ankle and Foot Muscles

Dorsiflexion. Tibialis anterior, extensor digitorum longus, peroneus tertius

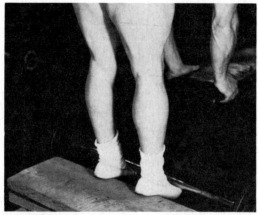

Figure 5.79. Ankle curls

Plantar Flexion. Gastrocnemius, soleus

Figure 5.80. Toe raises

Figure 5.81. Toe presses

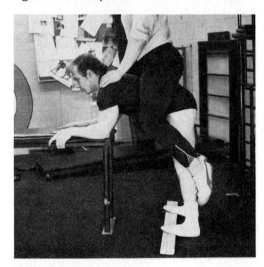

Figure 5.82. Donkey raises

Inversion and Eversion. Tibialis anterior, tibialis posterior, extensor digitorum longus, peroneus group. These movements, and related exercises, are generally done through remediation mandates, and need not be strengthened via specialized exercises for the normal person. If desired, however, simply walking on the inside and outside of the foot will suffice.

Exercises for the Muscles of the Wrist Joint and Hand

Forearm development, excepting muscles involved in elbow and radio-ulnar joint actions, depends on finger and wrist exercises. This is true since most of the major muscles acting on the fingers and wrists are located in the forearm. Long tendons attach to the individual joints. Generally, simply handling weights during other exercises is sufficient to force development of these muscles. However, a few specialized exercises may be helpful:

Figure 5.83. Thor's hammer

Figure 5.84. Wrist curls — reverse wrist curls may also be utilized.

Daily Dozen for Women

It is important to note that there are few special exercises just for women, with the exception of certain exercises specific to pregnancy. Women can and should perform the same types of resistance exercises as men for sport as well as for lifetime fitness. As we have mentioned, hormonal differences in women will preclude them from experiencing muscle hypertrophy to the degree that a man might. This is especially true with the torso musculature; so women can bury their fears of developing massive arms and shoulders, but instead can expect to become leaner and more trim with a proper personalized fitness program. Below is an example of 12 exercises which can be performed by a woman (or man) which will lead to an overall increase in muscle tone, an increase in strength, and a decrease in the ratio of fat to lean tissue. These should be performed three times per week, but may be performed four to five times per week if the resistances are kept low and the perceived exertion for each exercise deemed moderate.

Description of Exercises

1. *Half Squats:* Gluteus Maximus, Hamstrings, Quadriceps, Erector Spinal Group
   a. Position feet flat on the floor directly beneath the shoulder pads of the squat machine with the heels sixteen to eighteen inches apart and toes pointing outward at a 20° angle. A vertical squat machine with a shoulder attachment that is adjustable to varying heights is recommended. There are only a couple on the market at present. A machine is preferable to a barbell in a circuit program because of the quickness and ease of weight selection and because a machine can be used with relative safety and without the need for spotters.
   b. Adjust the height of the shoulder pads so that the upper and lower leg form an 80° angle when feet are positioned as described and the shoulders are pressed slightly into the shoulder pads. This is the starting position for the exercise, with back flat, feet flat on the floor, and hips six to eight inches behind the shoulders.

 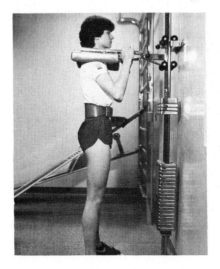

c. From this position tighten the back, hips, and legs, then begin to extend the hips and legs until reaching an upright position, but do not lock or hyperextend the knees.

d. Return to the start position, lightly touching the plates to the remainder of the weight stack, and return to an upright posture.

e. Exhale during the extension or upward portion of the exercise, and inhale on the way down (during the eccentric phase).

f. Remember to keep the back tight and flat at all times, and keep the head up.

2. *Back Press:* Pectoralis Major, Anterior Deltoid, Triceps

a. This exercise can be performed using a barbell or bench press machine.

b. Remove the bar from the standards, and hold it steady at arms length.

c. Lower the bar to the chest, usually at the level of the fifth rib, and immediately return the bar to its starting position by straightening the arms.

    d. The lifter should avoid bouncing the bar off the chest, or any uplifting of the hips off the bench.

    e. The bar should navigate a slight backward arc from the chest to a position above the eyes as the arms are extended.

3. *Calf Raises:* Gastrocnemius, Soleus, Peroneus Longus and Brevis, Tibialis Posterior, Flexor Digitorum Longus

    a. Position the balls of the feet over the rear edge of the toe board of the calf machine and place shoulders into the shoulder pads.

    b. Extend the legs and lift the weight stack to an erect position with knees locked.

    c. Lower the heels below the toe board to pre-stretch the calf muscles. Then extend the foot and raise the heel as high as possible maintaining straight knees.

    d. Return the heels to the starting position and repeat movement.

4. *Alternate Leg V-Ups:* Iliacus, Psoas Major and Minor, Pectineus, Rectus Femoris, Rectus Abdominis

   a. Begin in supine position with both arms overhead on floor.

   b. Flex the trunk, bring the arms up along with the trunk; simultaneously raising one leg so that both hands touch the foot or lower shin of the raised leg.

   c. Lower arms, trunk, and leg to the floor simultaneously and repeat the movement raising the alternate leg to meet the hands.

   d. Attempt to raise the leg to about a 60° angle and bring trunk and arms up to touch feet at that point.

   e. Exhale on the way up and inhale on the way down.

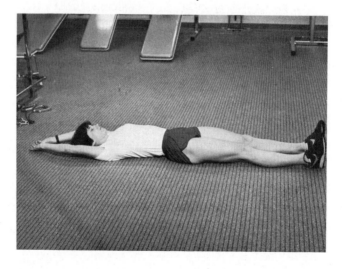

5. *Standing Dumbbell Press:* Deltoids (especially the lateral and anterior), Triceps, Serratus Anterior

    a. Begin by positioning two dumbbells at shoulder level, feet spread shoulder width, and legs straight.

    b. From this position you can either extend both arms simultaneously overhead, then lower the dumbbells to shoulder level; or you can first extend one arm, then extend the other as you are lowering the first to shoulder level. The latter is called an alternate dumbbell press; and the key to proper execution is to lower one dumbbell while simultaneously raising the other.

    c. If pressing both dumbbells together exhale during the press phase and inhale while lowering. If performing an alternate dumbbell press inhale during one repetition and exhale during another.

6. *Barbell Lunges:* Gluteus Maximus, Hamstrings, Quadriceps, Adductor Group
   a. Have spotters position a barbell (approximately 20% of bodyweight) on your shoulders. Bring the arms around behind the bar and rest the hands on the plates at both ends of the bar.
   b. Begin by stepping forward with the right foot approximately thirty to thirty-six inches and lowering the left knee to the floor as the right knee flexes.
   c. Forcefully push up and back extending the right leg and returning to the starting position.
   d. Repeat this movement with the left leg forward. Caution is recommended!

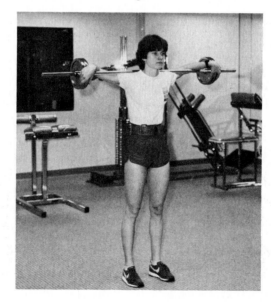

7. *Vertical Fly Machine:* Pectoralis Major, Anterior Deltoid

    a. Position yourself in the machine back against the back rest, forearms against the arm pads, and upper arms approximately horizontal. The machine will pull the elbows laterally and back so as to place the pectoralis major on stretch.

    b. Rotate the upper arms horizontally about the axis of the shoulder, pressing the elbows together, until the arm pads of the machine touch one another, exhaling during this phase.

    c. Return the arms to the starting position inhaling as you do this.

    d. Repeat.

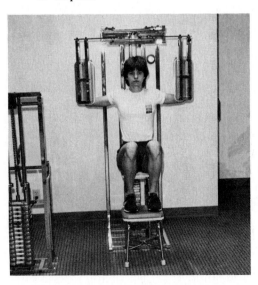 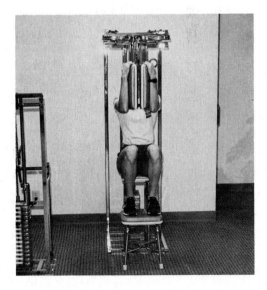

8. *High Pulls:* Erector Spinae Group, Gluteals, Quadriceps, Hamstrings, Gastrocnemius, Soleus, Trapezius, Deltoids, Biceps, Forearms

   a. Address the bar with feet twelve to fourteen inches apart, toes straight ahead, and shins within two inches of touching the bar.
   b. Reach down and grasp the bar firmly (palms down) with a shoulder width grip. At the same time assume a position with hips below shoulders, back flat, head up, arms straight, and feet flat.
   c. Tighten all muscles of back, hip, legs, and shoulders prior to beginning the exercise.
   d. Extend the hips, back, and legs forcefully lifting the bar off the floor vertically. During the lift, the hips should never raise up faster or sooner than the shoulders. In other words the angle of the torso to the leg should never decrease only increase. This assures that you are using leg and hip strength to start the bar moving.
   e. As the body approaches an erect position the bar is kept close to the body and the arms which have remained straight up to this point begin to flex; the shoulders are shrugged using the trapezius muscles, and the lifter raises up on the toes.
   f. The arms, shoulders, and trapezius muscles maintain the momentum imparted to the bar by the legs, hips, and back; and the bar is lifted vertically to approximately neck or chin level. At no time do the elbows snap under the bar as they would in a power clean. The weight is lowered to the floor in somewhat the reverse manner as it was lifted.
   g. As soon as the bar touches the floor it is lifted again.
   h. The best breathing pattern seems to be inhaling during the first part of the lowering phase and exhaling during the pulling or lifting phase.

9. *Twists on Decline Bench:* Rectus Abdominis, Internal Obliques, External Obliques

    a. Assume a seated position on decline bench with a wooden stick across the back of the shoulders, and arms wrapped around the stick from behind, resting atop the stick, and extended to the sides.

    b. Lean back until the torso reaches an angle of 90° to the bench top or slightly greater.

    c. Begin by twisting the torso first to one side as far as possible while maintaining the angle of the torso to the bench, and then to the other side.

    d. Rotate the head as the shoulders rotate so that the relationship of the head to the shoulders remains the same as it was at the start.

    e. Repeat.

10. *Lat Pulldowns:* Latissimus Dorsi, Teres Major, Rhomboids, Biceps, Sternal Pectoralis Major

    a. Sit on a stool or bench, or kneel on the floor below the high pulley station.

    b. Position your shoulders either directly under the bar or slightly in front of it.

    c. Take a wide grip on the bar (slightly more than shoulder width) and begin with arms straight.

    d. Flex arms and rotate scapulae so as to pull the bar down behind the neck touching the bar gently on or about the seventh cervical vertebra.

    e. Slowly allow the bar to raise so that the arms are once again extended overhead in the starting position.

    f. Repeat.

11. *Back Extensions:* Erector Spinae Group, Hamstrings Group, Gluteus Maximus, Trapezius, Rhomboids

    a. Position yourself on the back extension apparatus in a prone position, achilles tendons under the leg pads, navel approximately 4 inches in front of the leading edge of the padded surface.

    b. If you plan to use extra weight, we suggest an olympic plate held behind the head. If you do not intend to use extra weight clasp the hands behind the head.

    c. Lower your head and shoulders until your torso forms a 90° angle with your legs. At this point raise the head and shoulders so that the back is straight and parallel to the floor.

    d. Keep elbows back as you raise the torso, and look up with the head as the torso reaches parallel. This will exercise the trapezius and rhomboid muscles as well as the erector spinal group.

    e. Return to the starting position (torso flexed) and repeat.

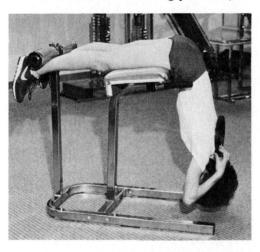 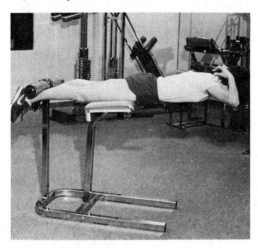

12. *Alternate Dumbbell Curls:* Biceps Brachii, Brachialis, Brachioradialis

    a. Stand erect, feet a comfortable and stable distance apart, legs straight, back straight; holding dumbbells in the anatomical position (arms down at the sides, palms facing forward).

    b. Flex the right arm raising the dumbbell to shoulder level, being sure to retain an erect posture with the back and avoid backward or lateral movement of the elbow.

    c. Lower the right hand while simultaneously flexing the left arm and raising the left dumbbell. The dumbbells should meet with both arms at a 90° angle as one goes up and the other goes down.

    d. When lowering a dumbbell the arm must reach a fully extended position.

    e. Repeat.

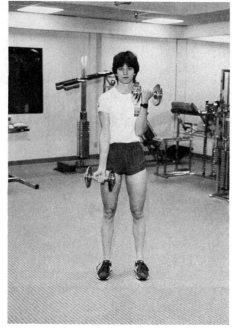

Conclusion

The student will find that each of the above exercises can be altered or adapted to fit individual needs. Many can be combined in a compound sequence. The important point to remember, regardless of one's specific goals, is that the principles of overload and isolation are absolutely essential in maximizing gains. So too is the SAID principle. The exercises catalogued here should, correspondingly, serve as a guide and model for exercise technique, but not to the exclusion of personal, sport-related needs.

One other point should be made regarding apparatus. If the student has the common problem of not being near a well-equipped facility, often he or she is forced to adapt many exercises for use with simple barbells, springs, dumbbells, or other commercially available devices. Generally, this is possible, but again, attempt to adhere to the basic principles of weight training as closely as available equipment will permit.

Nutrition for Health and Sport

Contents: *Determining Level of Underweight or Overweight*
Physiology of Losing and Gaining Weight
    Gaining Weight. Losing Weight.
Considerations of Sound Nutrition
Fats, Carbohydrates, and Protein
    Fats. Carbohydrates. Protein.
Vitamins, Minerals, and Water
Making Weight for Athletic Contests
Ergogenic Aids
    Amphetamines. Anabolic steroids. Caffeine. Nicotine. Alcohol. Aspartic acid.
    Alkalies. B_{15}. Pollen extract. Pain Killers. Disinhibition by conditioning.

6

The tremendous complexity of the biochemical mechanisms of the human body, coupled with environmental and psychological variables which are no less complex, precludes the possibility of stating in any exact terms just what constitutes a "sound" diet. There are, however, basic laws which govern energy balance that must be used in weight gain or loss endeavors. There are also basic physiological considerations involved in determining nutritional needs, although all one can hope for in this regard is to temper them with common sense—application of known information with self-knowledge is a must in developing a sound diet. This chapter will endeavor to present basic knowledge governing weight control, nutrition for health as well as sport, and will also speak to the most commonly used (and misused) food supplements and work-producing or ergogenic aids.

Determining Level of Underweight or Overweight

How often have you stepped on a scale and exclaimed, "Gee, I've gained weight?" Or, perhaps less frequently, "Gee, I've lost weight?" While one's weight may often indicate one's degree of leanness or lack of it, there is certainly a better indicator. One's weight says nothing of how much fat is present in comparison to one's lean body mass, and this is the critical question. Tables of average weights, such as are used by the armed forces or by insurance companies for selection or actuarial purposes, are relatively useless, for they do not account for individual differences with regard to bone density or muscle mass. They are nothing more than a manifestation of the common misconception which has been operative in this country for a long time, that weight determines fitness. The best method is to determine your fat-free weight and by subtraction calculate how much fat is present (your percent body fat).

There are many techniques presently in use in diagnosing overweight/obesity. Underwater weighing techniques make use of Archimedes' principle, wherein one's specific gravity is determined. Then, after accounting for one's residual lung volume, a corrected estimate of specific gravity is obtained. Tables have been developed to allow one to determine his/her percent of body fat from estimates of specific gravity. Underwater weighing techniques offer the best measure of percent body fat, but suffer the disadvantage of being time-consuming and requiring specialized equipment.

There are two other techniques which, while not as accurate as underwater weighing techniques, nonetheless offer fair approximations of one's percent body fat, and are much easier to administer. *Skinfold* estimates, calculated by the use of a caliper device, have been used successfully, and vary as little as ± 3% from measures derived by the underwater weighing technique. *Anthropometric* measures, which yield estimates of percent body fat varying ± 4% from underwater weighing measures are derived by measuring girths of various body parts. Both of these methods afford the fitness enthusiast or athlete information which will be invaluable in determining his/her degree of obesity, and are easy enough to use that simple weight watching should be excluded from its present level of importance. These techniques are presented in Chapter 7.

Exercise physiologists appear to be in agreement as to desired levels of body fat for average people. Ten to fourteen percent is ideal for young men, and for women it is slightly higher, around 18%–21%. While there are differences of opinion as to what level of body fat constitutes clinical obesity, averages for men are around 25% and for women around 32%–35%. Many athletes have been measured at values below 5%. While recommended minimums have not been established, it should be pointed out that some fat is necessary for padding around joints, lubrication between skin and muscle, and for insulation. A safe estimate might be in the area of 5%, but this proportion may vary depending upon one's somatotype, sex, and activity level. Table 6.1 describes some percent body fat averages for various sport participants.

Physiology of Losing and Gaining Weight

Calorie balance is the key to gaining and losing weight. When the caloric intake exceeds the energy expenditure, a positive energy balance exists, and that energy is stored as fat. Each pound of fat is capable of storing 3,500 calories. Thus, a positive energy balance of 3,500 kilocalories will result in one pound of fat being deposited. Conversely, a negative energy balance of 3,500 kilocalories will result in one pound of fat being used as energy.

Tabled below (Table 6.2) are approximate energy requirements of various types of activities. It should be clear that, in view of the amount of activity required to "burn off" one pound of fat, something more than merely exercising is called for. Prudent dieting is also a key to losing fat, and exercise is an aid. Furthermore, for reasons of psychological and social well-being, one should strive to eliminate excess body fat over a long period of time, rather than by potentially dangerous or discouraging crash diets.

Before concluding that exercise is not important, however, consider the following points. While it is neither desirable nor recommended to run the thirty-odd miles required to lose one pound of fat, running for one-half hour daily is equivalent to about a twenty-pound weight loss over a period of one year. Also, obese people (those in more serious need of weight loss) do not eat more with increased activity. On the contrary, their appetites usually decline with increased activity, further assisting in creating the desired negative energy balance.

Table 6.1. Percent Body Fat Averages of Various Sport Participants*

Designated Sport	Male %	Female %
Baseball/Softball	13	23
Basketball	9	23
Canoeing	12	—
Football	9.4–20	—
Gymnastics	5	15
Ice Hockey	9–13	—
Nordic Skiing	8	—
Ski Jumping	14	—
Soccer	9	—
Speed Skating	11	—
Swimming	5–9	15
Tennis	—	15
Track and Field		
Discus	16	25
Runners	5–13	7–18
Shot	16	28
Tri-Athletes	4–7	—
Volleyball	—	25
Weight Lifting		
Power	15	—
Olympic	12	—
Body Building	7	—
Wrestlers	5–11	—
Average	15–18	22–25

*Compiled averages from various sources by M. L. Krotee and F. C. Hatfield.

Recalling from the discussion on energy sources (Chapter 1), muscular energy is derived from the breakdown of organic compounds and glycogen which is stored in the muscle and liver. Glycogen storage results from the metabolic breakdown of fats, carbohydrates, and protein, the three major sources of calories. During periods of positive energy balance, fat tissue is synthesized in the liver and transported to various sites for deposit. During periods of negative energy balance, fat, generally from the last place it was deposited, is reclaimed for energy production. This "last on, first off" principle is the source of much discouragement among dieters, since fat is generally redeposited during weight gain in the areas (hips and midsection) where effort has been made to lose fat. These areas are generally the last places fat will be reclaimed from, accounting for their discouragement: Dieting prudently, (trimming 200–500 calories per day) and exercising regularly over a long period is the best alternative to rid oneself of these unwanted fat deposits.

Table 6.2. Energy Costs of Various Activities.*

Physical Activity	Estimated Kcal/hour
Archery	270
Badminton	400
Basketball	560
Billiards	235
Bowling	215
Bull Session	90
Calisthenics	200
Cleaning	185
Cooking	240
Cycling (5 mph)	300
Disco	450
Dressing	200
Driving to Class	180
Field Hockey	560
Gardening	295
Golf	340
Gymnastics	257
Jogging	750
Lying Quietly	80
Marathon Running	990
Playing Cards	140
Racquet Sports	870
Rowing (6 mph)	900
Running (7 minute mile)	950
Singing	120
Sitting in Class	90
Skating	470

*The estimated energy requirements are based on a 70 kg or 154 pound participant. The participant may add or subtract 10 Kcal per hour per activity for each 5 pounds that deviates from the 154 guideline. Remember age, sex, size in body area, nutritional patterns, skill, and the environment make the above Kcal count only an estimate.

Table 6.2—Continued

Physical Activity	Estimated Kcal/hour
Skiing (Nordic)	1080
Skipping Rope	800
Sleeping	70
Soccer	540
Softball	280
Squash	650
Studying/Reading	105
Swimming	500
Table Tennis	280
Television	90
Tennis	450
Volleyball	255
Walking to Class	300
Walking up Stairs	180
Washing and Shaving	150
Weight Training	550
Wood Chopping	560
Wrestling	790

Gaining weight. It should be clear that in order to gain weight (without increasing percent body fat), one must engage in some form of activity which produces muscular hypertrophy while at the same time limiting energy expenditure. The best available activity in this regard is weight training, particulars of which have been discussed in the preceding chapters. Many people, owing to relatively high metabolic rates, have difficulty in gaining weight. This has been found to be especially true of college students, since much psychological pressure from worrying about exams and the like contributes to tremendous levels of energy expenditure. Nervous temperament of this sort, over long periods, requires high amounts of energy. For these individuals a high food and calorie intake is often times very difficult to maintain but a 2500–3500 positive calorie balance over a week's time should place almost one pound on the body's frame. Table 6.3 indicates the recommended number of weeks required to gain muscle weight. Positive calorie balance and weight training must be employed together to achieve this type of observed weight gain.

Table 6.3. The Recommended Number of Weeks Required to Gain Muscle Weight

		10	20	30	40	50	60
Present	100	10	20	30	40	50	60
Lean	120	9.5	19	28.5	38	47.5	57
Body	140	9	18	27	36	45	54
Weight	160	8.5	17	25.5	34	42.5	51
(in Lbs.)	180	8	16	24	32	40	48
	200	7.5	15	22.5	30	37.5	45
	220	7	14	21	28	35	42
	240	6.5	13	19.5	26	32.5	39
	260	6	12	18	24	30	36
	280	5.5	11	16.5	22	27.5	33
	300	5	10	15	20	25	30
		5	10	15	20	25	30
				Increase in Pounds Desired			

Losing weight. Many research endeavors of the past two decades have pointed clearly to the fact that the primary cause of obesity is inactivity. While it is true that overweight people have a positive energy balance, it is also true that this positive balance stems from inactivity, not excessive caloric intake. Furthermore, crash diets and fasting methods are not recommended because much of the weight lost is due to a reduction of fluids and lean body mass—not adipose tissue. Research conducted in this regard indicates that about 65% of weight lost was from muscle tissue, while only 35% was due to fat loss.

From the foregoing discussion, it can be concluded that the best alternative for losing unwanted fat is to exercise vigorously each day and to count calories as well. Overly obese people have the particular problem involving possible damage to the cardiovascular system with too strenuous an exercise program, as well as the possibility of damaging connective tissues of joints due to extreme stress. Therefore, these people should solicit the advice of a physician and train under the watchful eye of someone trained in the art and science of exercise.

Recent research in methods of dieting have yielded some exciting concepts. It was found that rats gained more weight by eating their entire daily ration within two hours than did rats eating small amounts throughout the day. This method, when extended to human subjects, showed a similar trend. Obese patients fasted for forty-eight hours (apparently a practice designed to alter the current metabolic pattern), and then were fed 1,320 calories daily, spread over six meals. The proportions of fats, carbohydrates, and protein were 15%, 55%, and 30%, respectively. None of the patients complained of hunger, and weight losses of up to 100 pounds were reported. If any conclusion can be drawn from this research, it must be that gorging oneself at one or two meals per day is unwise, and skipping breakfast (common in the United States) is discouraged. The answer then is to eat more frequent but smaller meals.

Considerations of Sound Nutrition

Virtually all experts in nutrition recommend eating foods from a variety of sources. This practice, it is claimed, will allow the individual to obtain all the necessary vitamins, minerals, and energy sources needed for good health. The recommended sources include vegetables and fruits, grains (bread and cereal), dairy products, meat and fish.

In this country, as in no other, the food-fad business is booming, Faddists and food supplement companies, due to the tremendous marketability of health-giving products, have been quick to jump on the bandwagon slogan that the average American is malnourished. Using their products, which range from vitamins to wheat germ oil, bee pollen, protein, and ginseng root, they claim, will result in better health. It should be clear, however, that most of these exotic supplements are actually foods themselves, the nutritional benefits of which could be obtained far more inexpensively through other, more practical sources. Many nutritionists, exercise physiologists, and FDA officials spend a lot of time and money discouraging the use of these food sources. There is nothing inherently wrong with most of them—they are, in some cases, excellent sources of many beneficial nutrients. It is clear, however, that a sound diet can be achieved in virtually countless ways and through countless sources. The safest recommendation appears to be to eat a variety of the foods that you feel most comfortable with and can most easily afford, be the food source exotic or ordinary and include foods only from each of the above mentioned food groups.

The critical issue is that some Americans are deficient in one or more essential nutrients. A recent study involving Big Ten athletes has shown that over 35% of the athletes observed had diets deficient in vitamins A and C, and calcium. If generally health-conscious athletes' diets are deficient, it seems quite possible that the average American's diet is also suspect.

Many people, especially athletes, cling to the hope that by supplementing their normal diets with various types of vitamin pills and other nutrients, their health, and especially their performance, will increase. They use the supplements as sort of a "hedge" against illness—an insurance policy. Many people, particularly the people in the business of selling such supplements, claim that there is nothing wrong with this practice, while others, notably FDA people, have pointed out the hazards of toxicity effects of overuse of various substances. The point is, however, that there is no scientific evidence that supplementation of a nutritionally sound diet will improve sport performance. Those extra vitamin pills, or that heaping spoonful of wheat germ will not yield additional strength or stamina if one's diet already provides all of the essential nutrients.

Considering the importance of the big "if," it seems appropriate to supplement food intake with multi-vitamins or other nutrients during times one suspects his/her diet to be less than complete, and to disregard such practices when one's diet is sound. Many factors are involved in determining the completeness of one's diet, and the most important factors seem to be activity level and caloric intake.

The authors admit that behavior modification (change in behavior) concerning diet and nutrition is a slow and gradual adaptive process. But making appropriate alterations and incorporating them into constructive habits together with participation in regular physical activity will without question add significantly to your quality of life.

The nature of this text precludes delving into discussion on daily requirements of various nutrients. Rather, the reader is directed to any good nutrition text wherein such lists are generally available. A brief discussion on the three basic food sources, however, seems in order, including fats, carbohydrates, and protein.

Fats, Carbohydrates, and Protein

As discussed previously, fats, carbohydrates, and protein are the three major sources of one's caloric intake. Deciding on what proportions of the three sources would produce an optimum intake must involve considerations of one's activity level, and one's present percent body fat. Also, consideration must be given to identifying the best sources of the three substances.

Generally, by varying the proportion in favor of protein and carbohydrate (i.e. reducing the amount of fat in the diet), and increasing one's activity level, fat deposits will be recruited to supply the necessary energy for muscular contraction. However, should one wish to simply diet without additional energy expenditure, simply reducing the caloric intake proportionately from all three sources of calories appears appropriate. It is generally agreed that physical activity increases one's need for various nutrients, and by increasing one's intake of all foods in a balanced diet, this will be accomplished. If the activity is severe enough to stimulate muscular growth, more protein is required, but carbohydrate and fat intake should remain at a proportionate level also. Below are tables of recommended proportions suggested by various professional sources. While similarities exist in the proportions suggested, the differences speak to the fact that information on optimal dietary distribution of calories is still not conclusive (see Table 6.4).

The following guidelines should be adhered to in selecting food sources of fats, carbohydrates, and protein:

Fats. Saturated fats cannot combine with other substances in the body. A review of simple rules of chemistry tells one that when the molecular structure of a substance is such that all available bonds are filled, that substance becomes relatively incapable of reacting with other substances. Rancid or hydrogenated fat falls into this category. All ingested fat should ideally be fresh and unsaturated. Animal fat is not recommended, while most vegetable fats are. Fats should be derived from 10% saturated, 10% monosaturated and 10% polyunsaturated and represent about 30% of our diet instead of its current estimated 45%. As fats are rich sources of vitamins A, D, E, and K, contain linolenic acid (an essential fatty acid) and are also high in protein; they are an important part of your diet and should not be neglected.

While fat-free diets are not recommended since some fat is required in the metabolizing of carbohydrates, neither is a fat-rich diet. Too much fat has been linked with reduced endurance and muscular efficiency.

Carbohydrates. Of the three types of food, carbohydrates are the chief source of fuel for muscular contraction. Excellent sources of carbohydrates include most vegetables, whole grain bread, and fresh fruits, because these foods also contain many other essential nutrients. Sugar containing foods are generally taboo, because they offer very little in the way of additional nutrients, while complex and simple carbohydrates are recommended. Aside from the obvious problem of increasing body fat proportions, high-carbohydrate diets have been linked with hypoglycemia, a condition wherein low blood sugar results from increased insulin production.

Table 6.4. Calorie Sources and Recommended Proportions

Sources of Information	Percentage of Total Daily Kilocalories		
	Fat	Carbohydrate	Protein
H. A. deVries (exercise physiologist) Percentages for the average person	40	48	12
Suggested percentages for athletes in training	35	46	19
L. Morehouse and A. Miller (exercise physiologists) Suggested percentages for athletes	20	65	15
B. Starr (strength coach for pro football team)	15*	30*	55*
W. Thorpe (nutritionist) Athletes	30	58 15% — simple 43% — complex	12 1–1½ gm/kg body wt.
U.S. Dietary Goals Senate Select Committee on Nutrition and Human Needs	30	58	12
S. Williams (nutritionist) Athletes	35	46	19

*Percentages were extrapolated from other information.

Apparently, evidence is mounting to support the theory that sugar primes the pancreas to secrete more insulin, making the hypoglycemia worse. Low-carbohydrate diets, on the other hand, also appear often to be the culprit in conditions of low blood sugar. Low blood sugar causes fatigue of both the muscles and the nervous system. A fatigued nervous state results in loss of coordination and thus mechanical efficiency.

Many athletes have, in the past few years, utilized a form of glycogen supercompensation prior to an important athletic contest in an effort to increase endurance. "Glycogen loading" as it has become known, involves a schedule similar to the following:

Days Before the Contest	Fat	Carbohydrate	Protein
7	high	none	normal
6	high	none	normal
5	high	none	normal
4	none	high	normal
3	none	high	normal
2	none	high	normal
1	none	high	none

This regimen of glycogen loading is normally accompanied by an exercise regimen which stresses high-intensity workouts early, diminishing in intensity nearer the contest. Also, the activities should be specific to the contest requirements early, diminishing to general-type exercises nearer the contest. There is much evidence indicating that such a program is beneficial for aerobic activities, but appears to be of little benefit for anaerobic-type sports. Furthermore, since it requires other than recommended allowances of the three basic foods, such a diet should be followed only before important contests—probably less than three per year. The theory behind such a practice is that by depleting one's stores of glycogen, and then replenishing them through a high-carbohydrate diet, the body adapts by overcompensation in that greater than normal levels of glycogen are stored. It should be pointed out that such a regimen may be hazardous to some athletes, particularly those who are sensitive to fluctuations in blood sugar levels, such as diabetics or prediabetics. Also, the same hazards are associated with such a diet as discussed previously regarding carbohydrate-rich or carbohydrate-deficient diets.

Protein. As with fats and carbohydrates, there are good and poor sources of protein. Proteins are composed of amino acids. Ingested proteins are broken down to their constituent amino acids during digestion, and are then resynthesized in various locations throughout the body. Of the twenty-two known amino acids, nine cannot be synthesized in the body, and must be derived from other sources. These are called the *essential* amino acids.

Diets rich in milk, eggs, and meats are high in all of the amino acids, while many grains and vegetables lack some of the essential ones. Vegetarians must be especially careful to include a complimentary variety of leaves, grains, seeds, roots, vegetables, and fruit in their diet to derive these essential amino acids; and these complimentary protein sources should be consumed at the same meal. Unless essential amino acids are derived from other sources during the meal, the incomplete proteins are of restricted benefit.

Aside from some of the basic considerations mentioned above, it seems unnecessary to belabor the point of good nutrition. In any event, exercise is by far of greater concern in improving sport performance levels, especially when one's diet is reasonably sound. Simple tallying techniques will tell one which nutrients are missing from one's diet, and once identified, they should be added. Bear in mind, however, that most of the necessary nutrients for sound health are dependent upon one another, and should, therefore, be ingested together in proportionate measures. Appropriate proportions can be achieved by simply partaking in good variety of wholesome, fresh foods. To get started on the right track, the reader is advised to consume foods from the basic four food groups as follows: At least four servings from the daily vegetable and fruit group; two from the dairy group; at least two from the meat or protein group and at least four servings from the grains or bread and cereal group.

Vitamins, Minerals, and Water

Humans cannot survive on carbohydrates and fats alone as evidenced by research concerning protein on certain African populations. Just as protein has been found to be essential to balance the big three energy source structures, the nutrients contained in vitamins, minerals, and water are also essential in maintaining the various critical metabolic functions of the body. Weight training participants have frequently related the vitamin B complex as well as iron, potassium, and salt to sustained and vigorous participation. Often vitamins and minerals together with a strong mixture of protein supplements have been stuffed into the body in an injurious manner without the least bit of knowledge as to why or what their potential detrimental effects might be. Other than the replacement of these substances to insure normal functioning, there has been little medical evidence that hyperloading of any of the substances mentioned above contributes to performance as related to physical activity. Indeed,the participant, by simply eating foods such as oranges, bananas, and adding a little additional salt to your hamburger in most instances replaces or supplies the needed amount of the above commonly abused items. The authors highly recommend that the participant maintain a normal intake of between 55%–61% carbohydrates, 27%–33% fats, and 10%–14% protein and to consult a physician if for some reason the normal diet is to be disturbed.

Making Weight for Athletic Contests

For years it has been customary for athletes such as jockeys, wrestlers, weight lifters, and boxers to "sweat off" excess pounds in order to make the desired weight category. Generally, water losses of up to 5% of one's body weight can be tolerated without detrimental performance effects being noticed. Such a practice should be preceded by weeks of preparation, in that sweating out excess water disrupts the body's delicate electrolyte balance. Sodium and potassium salts are recommended as supplements to one's diet, in order that undue cramping during competition may be prevented.

The trend nowadays appears to be for the athlete to maintain his/her competition weight year-round, thereby eliminating such radical procedures and their attendant side effects. Studies performed on Russian and Bulgarian weight lifters have indicated that 3.5% losses of body weight will not harm performance; losses of about ten pounds per lift were noted when the athlete was required to lose 4.5%, and about twenty pounds at 5.5%.

It should be noted that the ratio of lean body weight and fat weight may often vary for different athletes. Football linemen require some fat for greater inertia and padding from severe blows. Swimmers need some fat for insulation from heat loss in the water. Gymnasts and wrestlers need little fat, as do most weight lifters and other athletes. Fat does not contribute to increased performance, in any event, nor does excessive water weight. Close tabs on one's diet throughout the year is definitely recommended for all classes of athletes, and maintaining an equitable ratio of lean body weight to fat weight is desirable. Should the athlete find it necessary to drop water weight immediately preceding a contest, the aforementioned guidelines should be adhered to. Further, be aware that fasting for periods of time will result in debilitating losses of lean body mass to a far greater extent than of fat weight, and is therefore not recommended under any conditions.

Ergogenic Aids

Ergogenic aids, or work-producing aids, are in widespread use in practically all quarters of the sporting world. Many are banned by various sport-governing bodies due to both health and ethical considerations. Others, perhaps as dangerous or potent as many of the banned drugs and substances, are not, due to their widespread usage by the general populace. The most common of the banned ergogens include amphetamines and anabolic steroids, while the legally used substances include caffeine, nicotine, alcohol, aspartic acid, various alkalinizers, vitamins, and extracts as well as many nonsubstantive procedures including music, hypnosis, and loud noises. In light of health and ethical considerations, stemming from both sound research as well as the lack of sufficient research, it is recommended that the athlete engage in the use of ergogens that are neither banned nor harmful if, in fact, they must be used at all. The following discussion of the commonly used ergogens should not be construed to be supportive of their use in sport and physical activity.

Amphetamines. A known stimulant, various forms of amphetamine have been found to increase athletic performance in endurance, strength, speed, and skill. Contradictory studies indicate that, in some cases, particularly involving unskilled or novice athletes, and athletes using such stimulants for the first time, they have either no effect or, in some cases, have detrimental effects upon performance. In either case, the dangers of using the drug are well-known, and for these reasons should be avoided: (1) they are addictive—athletes addicted to amphetamines perform poorly without them; (2) they block signals of impending muscular overexertion, thereby increasing the risk of serious injury; (3) vasoconstriction occurs while, at the same time, the force and rate of the heartbeat is increased; and (4) several cases of athletes collapsing (with, in some cases, ensuing death) from overdoses have been reported.

Anabolic steroids. Testosterone, the male hormone, has both androgenic effects as well as anabolic effects. While the androgenic component is responsible for producing masculine characteristics, the anabolic component is responsible for retention of ingested nitrogen necessary in the biosynthesis of protein. Synthetically produced anabolic steroids mimic the anabolic qualities of testosterone, thereby making it possible to recover more quickly from heavy exercise such as might be used in producing strength or hypertrophy. Since the recovery process is hastened, one can, theoretically, undergo heavy exercise more often, thereby speeding the process of muscle strength or size development. There is much contradictory evidence as to whether this drug is efficacious in its intended purpose. Many of the studies performed in this area, however, suffer from methodological flaws which tend to render them useless as sources of accurate information. Recent Eastern European studies have indicated their efficacy in the aforementioned regard, and have gone a step further by claiming that, under professional administration, they are not harmful. However, many other medical people have identified side effects that should be given consideration. They (steroids) have been found to be hepatic, carcinogenic, and responsible for undue edema, testicular shrinkage, and a host of other side effects. As with amphetamines, the traffic in steroids in the sporting community is very real, and until inexpensive and widely-administered control procedures similar to those in the recent World and Pan American Championships are implemented, will remain a problem. The reader is cautioned in the strongest terms against their use and is referred to Table 6.5 for the American College of Sports Medicine's position statement. If usage is still one's intent, at least consult a physician first.

Table 6.5. American College of Sports Medicine Position Statement on the Use
and Abuse of Anabolic — Androgenic Steroids in Sports

Based on a comprehensive survey of the world literature and a careful analysis of the claims made for
and against the efficacy of anabolic — androgenic steroids in improving human physical performance, it
is the position of the American College of Sports Medicine that:

1. The administration of anabolic — androgenic steroids to healthy humans below age fifty in medically
   approved therapeutic doses often does not of itself bring about any significant improvements in
   strength, aerobic endurance, lean body mass, or body weight.

2. There is no conclusive scientific evidence that extremely large doses of anabolic — androgenic
   steroids either aid or hinder athletic performance.

3. The prolonged use of oral anabolic — androgenic steroids (C_{17} alkylated derivatives of testosterone)
   has resulted in liver disorders in some persons. Some of these disorders are apparently reversible
   with the cessation of drug usage but others are not.

4. The administration of anabolic — androgenic steroids to male humans may result in a decrease in
   testicular size and function and a decrease in sperm production. Although these effects appear to
   be reversible when small doses of steroids are used for short periods of time, the reversibility of
   the effects of large doses over extended periods of time is unclear.

5. Serious and continuing efforts should be made to educate male and female athletes, coaches,
   physical educators, physicians, trainers, and the general public regarding the inconsistent effects of
   anabolic — androgenic steroids on improvement of physical performance and the potential dangers
   of taking certain forms of these substances, especially in large doses, for prolonged periods.

Caffeine. While caffeine is a strong mental stimulant, it also retards coordination. The
athlete engaged in skilled movements is well-advised to stay away from coffee or tea prior to
competition. Athletes engaged in activities that require little skill but high arousal have, on the
other hand, noted beneficial effects in performance. However, prolonged and heavy use of coffee
or tea has the debilitating effect of interfering with carbohydrate and protein metabolism, thereby
offering the risk of rendering training ineffective for strength or size gains. Furthermore, since
caffeine is suspected of having adverse effects on cardiovascular function, endurance athletes
are well-advised to reconsider its use.

Nicotine. It is certainly unnecessary to delve into the hazards of cigarette smoking at this
point in time. Objectively, however, many tobacco users appear to be relatively unaffected by
smoking. There is some evidence that as high a proportion as 37.5% of young men are, however,
sensitive to tobacco, and, in controlled tests of speed of movement, showed decrements in performance. It appears possible that, due to the addictive effects of prolonged use of tobacco,
some men (and presumably some women also) perform better after smoking. This effect may
be attributable to psychological reasons, however, rather than physical. The safest recommendation is to quit—performance increases attributable to smoking are, in any case, so slight as
to make any increases noted not worth the risk.

Alcohol. As tests on drivers have indicated, excessive doses of alcohol are detrimental to
performance and mental function. However, there is much evidence that small doses of alcohol
may be ergogenic in nature, providing that the activity about to be engaged in does not require
high levels of skill. One study indicated that a small dose of alcohol taken five to ten minutes

before a strength test increased performance for up to forty minutes, but caused a performance decline thereafter. Another study involving degree of work output found that up to 240 cc of beer or brandy taken immediately or up to four hours beforehand increased the performance levels of habitual drinkers, but was detrimental to the performances of nondrinkers. The same amount taken the night before caused a marked drop in performance. There have been studies indicating that small doses of alcohol cause a decrease in O_2 debt as well as increased endurance in chilled muscles. Others show no such effects. Recent studies indicate that people who drink small doses daily over a lifetime tend to live longer than nondrinkers. While no reasons were presented for this surprising data, it appears possible that the depressant effect of the alcohol calms or lulls the user into a better night's sleep.

Whatever the case may be, as in smoking, noted increases in performance are slight at best, and the potential side effects of alcohol usage, particularly the addictive effect, warrant careful consideration on the part of the user. Furthermore, there is some evidence accumulating that excessive alcohol usage interferes with the metabolism of protein, a consideration which should be attended to by the athlete wishing to train for strength or hypertrophy.

Aspartic acid. Aspartic acid is involved in the metabolism of carbohydrates and protein. This function ultimately results in the formation of energy from carbohydrate breakdown. Studies have indicated that aspartic acid, in the form of potassium and magnesium asparates, is beneficial in offsetting fatigue, particularly in untrained subjects. Apparently, administration of aspartic acid had little effect on trained subjects. Further, little benefit was noted in the performance levels of strength athletes using aspartic acid. Since aspartic acid salts are generally considered a "food" rather than a drug, it appears that sensible use of this compound may, in some cases, be beneficial.

Alkalies. When work progresses beyond aerobic capacity, lactic acid becomes the end product of metabolism. The presence of lactic acid drastically inhibits the ability to accumulate an O_2 debt. However, if the blood is made more alkaline, lactic acid is neutralized, thereby delaying exhaustion. Numerous studies have reported increases of up to 100% in work capacity following a program of blood alkalinizing (ingestion of sodium citrate, sodium bicarbonate, and potassium citrate immediately following meals). Noted side effects, normally avoidable if the alkaline solutions are ingested after meals, include nausea, abdominal discomfort, and diarrhea. Also, alkalosis, a condition of developing too high a level of alkalinity in the blood, has been found to result in overexcitability of the nervous system, a condition which can cause muscular tetany. Clearly more research is needed in this domain.

Vitamin B15. A sometimes ingested substance also known as pangamic acid or dimethyl that as in Vitamin E has been reported to improve endurance capacity. The American Council on Science and Health has noted that B15 is not to be confused with a vitamin and further research indicated that B15, Vitamin E, as well as other nutritional supplements such as gelatin, honey, lecithin, and wheat germ have no benefit effect on physical performance. Stay away from B15!

Pollen Extract. Bee pollen extract has been marketed for sometime postulating benefits for various components of the blood thereby increasing endurance. No research has been found to support this contention so don't get stung on the way to the market!

Pain Killers. All forms of local analgesics (pain killers) have been observed in use for the last two decades. Chemical pain killing substances and remedies such as dimethyl sulfoxide (DMSO) should be treated very carefully or side effects may persist. At any rate a physician's prescription and clearance concerning the above is always recommended.

Disinhibition by conditioning. While one's *true* physical capacity may be limited by physiological conditions, one's normally observed maximum physical capacity is determined by acquired inhibitions. Loud noises, music, yelling, and other methods including hypnosis have been shown to be capable of increasing performance in strength and endurance feats. Apparently, such practices have a disinhibitory effect on the organism. It is interesting that such conditioning techniques are not more widely used in sport. In light of their seeming innocuous nature, perhaps they should be, especially considering that performance increases of from 7.4% to 26.5% have been noted through such procedures. A common anecdote is often told of the mother, in a moment of desperation, lifting a rolled-over car from her pinned child. Many such stories are confirmed, attesting to a very important conditioning component to performance. Far more research is needed in this intriguing area.

Techniques of Progress Assessment

Contents: *Simple Methods of Determining Percent Body Fat*
Skinfold Method. Anthropometric Method.
Determining White Versus Red Fiber Ratio
Estimating Physical Work Capacity
Test for General Fitness

7

In weight training, as in any worthwhile endeavor, efficiency in terms of time expenditure and derived benefits is desirable. Frequently, although one has arduously and meticulously adhered to basic principles such as those described in the preceding chapters, plateaus are reached, beyond which the exerciser cannot progress. Also problems of boredom, overtraining, diet, health, and injuries often tend to prohibit gains. In the interest of efficiency, reasonably complete record-keeping is recommended to all fitness enthusiasts and athletes alike. Problems are easily identified and training procedures which are contributing positively or negatively toward attainment of one's training objectives, once recorded, can be referred to without reliance on memory. Past performance levels can be related to preceding training practices to insure that future training—and subsequent performance levels—are maximized. Such objectivity is lost if memory is relied upon as the sole source of information regarding training and performance.

On the other hand, such record-keeping and measurement procedures would tend to be a hindrance, more than an aid, if they required extensive time, effort, or apparatus. There must be objectivity in records and measurements analysis, true, but elaborate equipment and time consuming methods of measurement and record-keeping are not necessary. The remainder of this chapter deals with simple, but reasonably effective and objective methods of progress assessment for the weight training enthusiast. Also included are samples of graphs, workout logs and norms for strength, endurance, and general fitness. Periodic self-testing will give the trainee an objective gauge by which to judge his/her progress, and record-keeping will supply the reference tool necessary in adjusting one's regimen when progress stalemates.

Simple Methods of Determining Percent Body Fat

As noted in the previous chapter, estimating one's ratio of lean versus fatty weight is desirable, considering the inherent dangers of excessive obesity. Two simple methods are recommended, involving skinfold estimates and anthropometric measures, respectively.

Skinfold method. Due to inherent sex differences relative to fatty deposits, it is necessary to use separate estimating procedures for men and women. The two methods are described below. To estimate one's percent body fat by the described method, both a tape measure and a skinfold caliper are required. There are many such methods available, most of which are suitable for classroom use. The critical aspect of such techniques lies in the careful manipulation of the calipers—an experienced technician should be available to take the required readings.

$$\text{Men: Body density} = 1.1043 - 0.001327 \, (\text{thigh skinfold}_{mm})$$
$$- 0.00131 \, (\text{subscapular skinfold}_{mm}).$$

Once one's body density is computed, use the obtained value in determining the percentage of body fat, as follows:

$$\text{Percent body fat} = 100(4.570)/\text{body density}_{gr/ml} - 4.142$$

$$\text{Women: Body density} = 1.0852 - 0.0008 \, (\text{suprailiac skinfold}_{mm})$$
$$- 0.0011 \, (\text{thigh skinfold}_{mm})$$

Upon determining one's body density, compute percent body fat, using the same equation listed above.

Nomograms located in Tables 7.1 (men) and 7.2 (women) illustrate an alternative method to assist in determining your percent body fat. A ruler and accurate skinfold measure are a must. Table 7.3 enables you to identify where you stand in regard to a compiled chart of percent body fat norms.

Table 7.1. Nomogram for Prediction of Percent Body Fat for Men

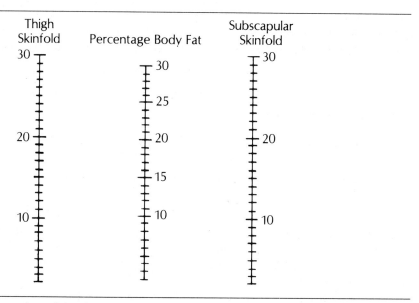

Tables 7.1 and 7.2. Nomograms for prediction of percent body fat. (From Sloan A. W. and J. B. de V. Weir. *Journal of Applied Physiology,* 28:221-222, 1970.)

Table 7.2. Nomogram for Prediction of Percent Body Fat for Women

| Suprailiac Skinfold | Percentage Body Fat | Triceps Skinfold |

Anthropometric method. Again, different procedures must be employed in determining percent body fat for men and women. Illustrated below is one sample method which is easily administered. All that is required is a tape measure. Caution must be used in assuring that the tape is held at a uniform tension, and positioned according to prescribed specifications.

$$\text{Men: Lean body weight} = 94.42 + 1.082 \,(\text{body weight nude}_{lbs})$$
$$- 4.15 \,(\text{waist girth at umbilicus}_{inches}).$$

Then, compute percent body fat as follows:

$$\text{Percent body fat} = \frac{\text{body weight} - \text{lean body weight} \times 100}{\text{body weight}}$$

$$\text{Women: Lean body weight}_{kg} = 8.987 + 0.732 \,(\text{weight}_{kg})$$
$$+ 3.786 \,(\text{wrist diameter}_{cm})$$
$$+ 0.434 \,(\text{forearm circumference}_{cm}).$$

The tape should be positioned over the widest points of the wrist and forearm, respectively, in obtaining accurate measures. Diameter is computed by dividing circumference by 3.14 *(Pi)*. Convert LBW_{kg} to LBW_{lbs} by multiplying $\text{LBW}_{kg} \times 2.2$. Then compute percent body fat as described above(men).

An alternative estimation procedure for women is as follows:

Table 7.3. Estimated Percent Body Fat Norms for the Normal Population*

	Men (%)	Women (%)
Athletic (low)	5–9	7–15
Athletic (average)	10–14	16–21
Average	15–18	22–25
Above Average (plump)	19–21	26–28
Too High	22–24	29–31
Obese	25+	32–35+

*Compiled from various sources by M. L. Krotee and F. C. Hatfield.

Determining White Versus Red Muscle Fiber Ratio

One might query as to the relevance of obtaining information relative to the ratio of white (fast-twitch) versus red (slow-twitch) muscle fiber he/she has. Recall (from Chapters 1 and 2) that white fiber is directly related to power and speed of movement, while red fiber is related to muscular endurance. While the total mass of white or red fiber can be changed through hypertrophy training, the number (or ratio) of white and red fibers is an inherited trait and cannot be changed. For one to be truly objective in assessing his/her capabilities in sport, particularly at the championship livel, such information can be useful in either selecting a sport within which the chances of success will be maximized, or in the construction of a suitable training regimen designed to yield maximal benefits in one's chosen specialty.

The clinical method of determining one's white/red fiber ratio is by extracting muscle biopsies, freezing them, staining and slicing them for microscopic scrutiny. However, recent research has provided a far simpler (although somewhat limited) method. By simply determining one's vertical jump ability, an estimate of the white/red ratio can be derived. This technique may be limited, however, by the extent of prior training effect. That is, an athlete who specifically trained for white fiber development, although having a higher proportion of red fibers, may do as well or better than an untrained athlete with the opposite white/red fiber ratio. For estimation purposes, however, it appears better suited than the alternative biopsy technique. Dr. James Councilman, Indiana University's well-known swimming coach, in collaboration with Dr. David Costill, Director, Ball State University's Human Performance Laboratory, have provided the following classifications, derived from testing both track and field athletes as well as swimmers. The classifications shown are for swimmers, but similar classifications can be made for runners and other athletes.

Table 7.4. Vertical Jump Method of Classifying Endurance Versus Sprint Swimmers.

Vertical jump of 9–22 inches: long distance swimmers (400–1500 meters);

Vertical jump of 20–24 inches: middistance swimmers (400–800 meters);

Vertical jump of 23–26 inches: long sprint swimmers (100–200 meters);

Vertical jump of 25–31 inches: short sprint swimmers (50–100 meters).

As one can see, overlap may occur between separate areas. Obviously, many other factors, such as mechanical efficiency of lever systems, technique, and especially motivation, must be accounted for in applying such a classification system. The reader is urged to reread the first two chapters of this text for purposes of putting the whole matter of the significance of red/white fiber ratio into its proper perspective.

The implication of the above classification is that swimmers with a low-vertical jump have a predominance of red fiber, accounting for their lack of power and greater endurance. Conversely, swimmers with a high-vertical jumping ability have a predominance of white muscle fiber, accounting for their greater power. The important point to remember is that however motivated or however highly skilled an athlete may become, it will be exceedingly more difficult for them to successfully engage in a power event if their musculature is predominantly red fiber; and it will be equally difficult for the athlete whose muscles are mostly white fiber to succeed in endurance activities.

To determine one's vertical jump ability, stand beside a wall and mark (with chalk) the highest point of reach. Then, without stepping, running, or swinging the arms (leave the unused arm at the side), jump as high as possible and mark the highest point of reach. Simply measuring the distance between the two marks will yield one's vertical jump distance. Take the best of three attempts. Don't cheat—stepping or swinging the arms tends to invalidate the test.

Estimating Physical Work Capacity

An easily administered test for determining one's physical work capacity (PWC) is afforded by the Harvard Step Test. This test is a moderately good estimator of PWC, having an error of prediction of maximal oxygen consumption of ±12.5%. It is based on the principle that the greater one's PWC, the greater the proportion of cardiac cost paid during exercise. In other words, the greater one's PWC, the smaller the O_2 debt to be paid during recovery.

The score, which is nothing more than an arbitrarily devised scale, should become progressively higher with training (aerobic). The following standards apply: below 50—poor; below 80—average; below 110—good; above 110—excellent. The user of this test is encouraged to complete five minutes of testing. However, should the test become so fatiguing as to be dangerous or incapacitating, stop, and apply the required heart rate measurement in the appropriate time-scale row. The specifications for testing are as follows: bench height—20 inches; 30 step-ups per minute; pulse taken at the carotid artery (right side of neck) for a 30 second

Table 7.5. Harvard Step Test Scale

Test Duration: Minutes	Total Heart Beats Taken 1–1½ Minutes After Test											
	40–44	45–49	50–54	55–59	60–64	65–69	70–74	75–79	80–84	85–89	90–94	95–99
3–3½	84	75	68	62	57	53	49	46	43	41	39	37
to 4	97	87	79	72	66	61	57	53	50	47	45	42
to 4½	110	98	89	82	75	70	65	61	57	54	51	48
to 5	123	110	100	91	84	77	72	68	63	60	57	54
5 min.	129	116	105	96	88	82	76	71	67	63	60	56

time period, which extends from 1–1½ minutes after test. After doing 30 step-ups per minute for five minutes, sit down, wait one minute, and count the numnber of times your heart beats in 30 seconds. Apply this number to the scale above to derive your PWC score. For example if you bench stepped for 4½ minutes and recorded a post test heart beat of 46 your PWC score would be 98 which indicates a "good" rating.

Test for General Fitness

Physical fitness, as the reader no doubt has concluded at this point in the present text, is a highly personalized matter. In Chapter 2, many of the factors that are involved in sporting prowess were discussed, and are generally the same in regard to overall fitness. However, many of these factors are specific to particular sports, to specific lifestyles and needs, and may not necessarily be desirable attributes in certain circumstances. The reader is left to decide what components of physical fitness are important to him/her, and to strive to achieve them. The following physical fitness test, then, is not a definitive test of fitness. Rather, it is meant to be a guide or reference point for the user. The test is not complete. Items such as power, agility, coordination, and related items such as balance, body composition, and posture are omitted. To obtain a true picture of one's state of fitness would require exceedingly long and tiring tests of individual attributes. The present test involves only those items deemed most commonly sought. Should testing in other areas be desired, the reader is referred to Krotee and Hatfield's *Theory and Practice of Physical Activity.*

The test. This test is designed to measure five attributes of physical fitness. The following directions are designed to enable you to administer the test to yourself or to another person. Read these directions carefully and observe the demonstrations given by your instructor so that you will be able to receive a reliable evaluation of your fitness status. The norms provided in Table 7.6 are for men with the exception of the twelve minute run.

Table 7.6. Physical Fitness Test Norms – Men and Women*

The following norms are expressed in percentile ranks. This means that a person scoring at a given rank did as well, or better than, that percent of people who have taken this test at the completion of this course. For example, a percentile rank of 70 means one did as well or better than 70% of the students who have taken this test. These norms are based on scores recorded at the end of a one-semester conditioning course.

Percentile Rank	Grip (lbs.)	Sit Ups (no.) 2 minutes	Weight Hold (seconds)	Push-ups (no.)	Flexion (inches)	Twelve Minute Run	1 1/2 Mile Run	Fitness Rating
100	160	97	115 or above	40+	+9	2 miles (2.0)		
95	148	94	85–114	38	+8	–		Superior
90	137	91	75–84	35	+7	–		
85	130	89	70–74	32	+6	over 1.74 (1.65)	10:15	
80	125	88	65–69	29	+5	1.74 (1.64)	10:16	
75	120	85	60–64	26	–	–		Above
70	118	83	–	23	+4	–		Average
65	115	82	–	20	–	Over 1.50 (1.35)	12:00	
60	113	80	55–59	18	–	1.50 (1.34)	12:01	
55	110	79	50–54	16	+3	–		Average
50	106	77	–	14	–	–		
45	104	75	45–49	12	–	–		
40	102	74	–	10	+2	Over 1.25 (1.15)	14:30	
35	100	72	40–44	8	–	1.25 (1.14)	14:31	Below
30	98	70	–	7	–	–		Average
25	95	68	–	6	+1	Over 1.0 (.95)	16:30	
20	93	66	35–39	5	–	1.0 (.94)	16:31+	
15	88	64	30–34	4	0	–		Poor
10	83	60	25–29	3	–1	–		
5	75	54	20–24	2	–2	.75 or under (.65)		

*Women's norms in parentheses.

159

Muscular Strength and Endurance

Hand Grip — Isometric (norms provided)

Purpose: To measure the strength of your grip, an indicator of total body strength.

Equipment: Hand dynamometer.

Procedure: Adjust the grip to your hand size. Set maximum pointer indicator at 20 pounds (not zero). Grip dynamometer in dominant hand, squeezing it with maximum force. The arm may remain stationary or move slowly (no rapid movement permitted), but neither arm nor instrument may touch any other part of the body or another object. Squeeze as hard as possible, relax, and squeeze again (two trials).

Scoring: The maximum number of pounds of force exerted by your squeeze will be recorded on the dial. Record to the nearest pound on your score card.

Sit-ups (norms provided)

Purpose: To measure the endurance of the abdominal muscles.

Equipment: Mats and watch.

Procedure: Lie on your back with legs straight and arms extended overhead. Knees are bent until feet can be placed flat on the mat (do not tuck heels close to buttocks). A partner kneels on floor at your feet holding down your insteps with their hands (partner should not kneel or sit on your feet, but exert enough pressure with the hands to hold feet down). On the starting signal, swing your arms forward and flex your trunk until you can touch the hands of the partner. After touching, return to the supine position, touching *both* hands to the mat. Action is repeated as many times as possible in the minute time period. Partner should move your feet during the test so as to keep the distance between the feet and buttocks relatively constant.

Scoring: Each correctly executed sit-up is counted out loud by the partner and the total number executed is recorded. Time is two minutes for men, one minute for women.

Flexed Arm Hang (no norms provided)

(Alternate Test for Women)

Purpose: To measure the endurance of the muscles in the arm and shoulder girdle.

Equipment: Horizontal bar and stop watch.

Procedure: Subject jumps and grasps the bar with the hands, palms toward face, approximately shoulder width apart. The body position is adjusted so that the bar is at chin level but the chin is not to be over or touching the bar. No kicking of leg or bending knees is permitted. If the body is swinging on the bar, a partner must stop it. A stop watch is started as soon as the subject is in the correct position. The timer calls off each second of time. The subject hangs in the prescribed position as long as possible. Time stops when the top of the subject's head drops below the bar.

Scoring: A partner should note the last second called off by the timer before the head drops below the bar and record this as the score.

Weight Hold (norms provided)

Purpose: To measure the endurance of the arm and wrist muscles.

Equipment: Weight and timing devices (60 lb. barbell for men, 30 lb. barbell for women)

Procedure: Stand against wall with feet six inches from wall and buttocks, upper back and elbows touching wall. A partner lifts the weight to a position in front of your chest. You grasp the weight (palms up) so the elbow is bent at a 90° angle or slightly higher. On the starting signal, your partner will release the weight. You hold it as long as possible at the 90° angle.

Scoring: When either arms drops below the 90° angle, the elapsed time is recorded to the nearest second. Maximum two minutes.

Push-up Test (norms provided)

Purpose: To measure the strength and endurance of the arm and shoulder extensors.

Equipment: 16–18 inch bench—women; no equipment—men.

Procedure: Assume a front leaning nest position with the hands on the floor (or bench) directly below shoulders, body straight, feet on floor. Bend elbows so body is lowered toward floor (bench) and touch chest, pushing back up to leaning position immediately with a straight body. No rest or sagging of body is permitted. Do as many as you can.

Scoring: Each time you perform one complete push-up starting in the up position, going down and back to the up position, one is scored. If your body sags or rests on the mat (at all), ½ push-up is scored, and after two such push-ups, the test is terminated.

Isometric Wall Sit (no norms provided)

Purpose: To measure the isometric endurance of the leg extensors (quadriceps).

Equipment: Stop watch, unobstructed wall space.

Procedure: Stand with the back and buttocks against wall. Move feet slowly away from wall, bending the knees and hips so that you slide down to a "sitting" position with the heels directly below the knees and the thighs parallel to the floor with a 90° angle at the knee and hip joint, and with the back pressed tightly against the wall (as if someone had just pulled a chair out from under you). Hold this position *without* placing the hands on the thighs as long as possible.

Scoring: Score is the time to the nearest second the position was held.

Anaerobic Fitness/Muscular Power Assessment

Vertical Jump: (no norm provided; see Lewis Nomogram in Table 7.7)

Purpose: To measure leg muscle power and body coordination.

Equipment: Same as described earlier in the chapter.

Procedure and Scoring

An easy method to assess your anaerobic fitness/power is by determining your vertical jumping distance and employing the Lewis Nomogram developed by the Office of Naval Research and located in Figure 7.7. To determine your vertical jumping distance or standing jump and reach measurement, simply stand with both heels on the ground and reach vertically with outstretched arms. Then jump three times measuring the distance from the standing reach mark to the standing jump mark. Take the average of the three jumps and just connect a straight edge from the nomogram distance column to the body-weight column which will supply you with your power in both kg-m/sec and ft-lb/sec. To convert these measures to horsepower (HP) multiply by .013 or .0018 respectively.

Flexibility

Bend and Reach Test (norms provided)

Purpose: To measure the flexibility of the trunk and lower back.
Equipment: Bench and measuring board.
Procedure: Stand on the bench with both feet touching the supporting brace of the board. Bending at the waist with the knees straight, reach with both hands (no leaning) as far down the scale as possible. Hold the lowest point for two seconds (no bobbing).
Scoring: The lowest point on the scale that can be reached and held for two seconds is noted by a partner. Score to the nearest inch (minus above toe level, plus below this mark).

Circulatory Respiratory Endurance

Twelve Minute Run (norms provided)

Purpose: To measure circulatory, respiratory endurance.
Equipment: Measured running area and timing device.
Procedure: On a given signal, begin jogging from a marked standing point. Your instructor will call off the time each minute. A partner will count the number of laps or distance completed in twelve minutes.
Scoring: Record the distance covered in terms of laps and fractions of laps completed when time has stopped.

Bench Step Test (no norms provided)

Purpose: To measure the anaerobic and short-term aerobic endurance capacity of the circulatory-respiratory system.
Equipment: Six inch step benches, stop watch.
Procedure: Stand facing the bench with a partner seated behind you. On the "Go" signal, begin stepping up onto the bench with both feet, and off the bench, i.e., up right, up left, down right, down left. Continue as rapidly as possible for two minutes.
Scoring: Score one for each time both feet are placed on top of the bench. Also see Harvard Step Test.

Table 7.7. The Lewis Nomogram for Determining Anaerobic Power. Adapted from Fox, E. L., and Mathews, D. K. *Interval Training,* Philadelphia: W. B. Saunders Company, 1974, p. 258.

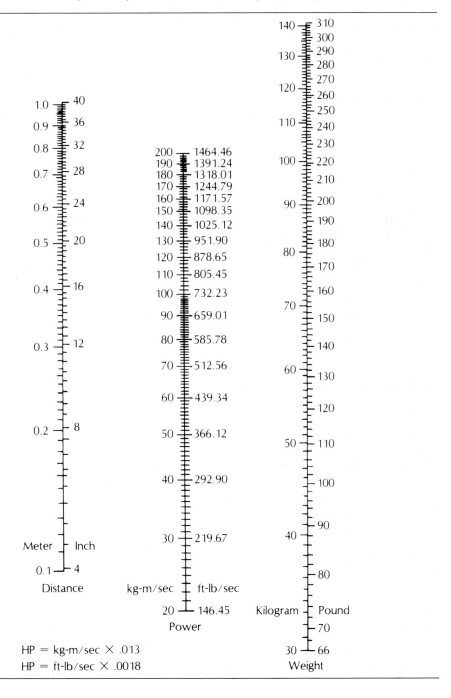

HP = kg-m/sec × .013
HP = ft-lb/sec × .0018

The remainder of this chapter is a compilation of format pages including workout logs, measurement charts, and norms for selected exercises. These exercises, for which norms are provided, should be done according to the specifications presented in the preceding chapter. Do each for one maximal repetition (1-RM) in strict fashion to derive the appropriate percentile ranking. Warm-up thoroughly before attempting a 1-RM. Also, be sure to refer to the appropriate table, as there are different tables for each body weight category. Students interested in overall fitness should strive to increase proficiency in those exercises in which they scored low. Bear in mind that these 1-RM scores are indicators of the involved muscles' strength, and as such should not be used for estimating other parameters such as muscular endurance or power.

The logs and measurement charts are provided as references for the trainee so that he/she can, in as efficient a manner as possible, record progress and be able to refer to prior training records to rectify/alter current training procedures for maximal benefit.

Table 7.8. 1-RM (one repetition with maximum) Strength Norms for College Men*

Sit-ups: Lying on floor with heels near buttocks (knees bent), and with feet secured, place weight behind head and sit up until elbows touch knees.

Curl: Leaning against wall, feet placed about 12–15 inches away from wall, curl bar to shoulders.

Upright row: Without swinging bar, and with a close grip, pull bar to chin.

Standing press: Without back lean, press bar from shoulders to overhead position.

Bench press: Lower bar to chest, pause, and press bar overhead without arching back or moving feet.

Deep knee bend (squat): Standing upright with the bar on the shoulders, squat down until thighs are flexed at approximately a 100° angle, then return to the upright position. Caution and a spotter is recommended.

Bent over row: Bending forward with back parallel to floor, put bar to chest, without jerking the bar or raising the body.

Back raise: With bar on back and knees very slightly flexed, bend forward until torso is parallel with the floor, and raise back up to an erect position. This is a potentially dangerous exercise, and extreme care should be exercised when performing a 1-RM. Warm-up and trained spotters are recommended.

---

*Norms for College Age Men in Selected Weight Exercises by R. A. Berger, 1970. Reprinted by permission of the author.

BODYWEIGHT CLASS 120–129 lbs.
1—RM

Sit-up (weight behind head)	Curl	Upright Rowing	Standing Press	Bench Press	(Squat) Deep Knee Bend	Bent Over Rowing	Back Raise	Standard Score†	Percentile‡
70 (42)	107.5(64.5)*	120 (72)	155(93)	170(102)	255(153)	185 (111)	215(129)	100	100
65 (39)	105 (63)	117.5(70.5)	150(90)	165(99)	245(147)	182.5(109.5)	210(126)	95	99.9
62.5(37.5)	107.5(61.5)	115 (69)	145(87)	160(96)	235(141)	180 (108)	205(123)	90	99.8
60 (36)	100 (60)	112.5(67.5)	140(84)	155(93)	225(135)	170 (102)	200(120)	85	99.4
57.5(34.5)	97.5(58.5)	110 (66)	135(81)	150(90)	220(132)	165 (99)	195(117)	80	98.4
55 (33)	95 (57)	107.5(64.5)	130(78)	145(87)	210(126)	157.5(94.5)	190(114)	75	96.2
52.5(31.5)	92.5(55.5)	105 (63)	125(75)	140(84)	200(120)	150 (90)	185(111)	70	90.3
50 (30)	90 (54)	102.5(61.5)	120(72)	135(81)	190(114)	140 (84)	180(108)	65	84.2
45 (27)	85 (51)	100 (60)	115(69)	130(78)	180(108)	135 (81)	175(105)	60	75.8
42.5(25.5)	82.5(49.5)	95 (57)	110(66)	125(75)	170(102)	127.5(76.5)	170(102)	55	64.0
40 (24)	80 (48)	90 (54)	105(63)	120(72)	160(96)	120 (72)	165(99)	50	50.0
37.5(22.5)	77.5(46.5)	85 (51)	100(60)	115(69)	150(90)	112.5(67.5)	160(96)	45	36.0
35 (21)	75 (45)	80 (48)	95(57)	110(66)	140(84)	105 (63)	155(93)	40	24.2
30 (18)	70 (42)	77.5(46.5)	90(54)	105(63)	130(78)	100 (60)	150(90)	35	15.8
27.5(16.5)	67.5(40.5)	75 (45)	85(51)	100(60)	120(72)	90 (54)	145(87)	30	9.7
25 (15)	65 (39)	72.5(43.5)	80(48)	95(57)	110(66)	85 (51)	140(84)	25	3.8
22.5(13.5)	62.5(37.5)	70 (42)	75(45)	90(54)	100(60)	80 (48)	135(81)	20	11.6
20 (12)	60 (36)	68.5(40.5)	70(42)	85(51)	95(57)	75 (45)	130(78)	15	.6
17.5(10.5)	57.5(34.5)	65 (39)	65(39)	80(48)	85(51)	70 (42)	125(75)	10	.2
15 (9)	55 (33)	62.5(37.5)	60(36)	75(45)	75(45)	65 (39)	120(72)	5	.1
12.5(7.5)	52.5(31.5)	60 (36)	55(33)	70(42)	65(39)	60 (36)	115(69)	0	0

*Female Estimates: May be found in parentheses and 60% may be employed in other bodyweight classes present.
†Standard Score: This score indicates the participant's relative position on the normal curve, with a standard deviation of 7 points.
‡Percentile: This score indicates the percentage of participants that fall below the lifters 1-RM performance.
Norms: Gathered from over 3,000 college-aged males following a ten week weight training program.

BODYWEIGHT CLASS 130–139 lbs.
1-RM

Sit-up (weight behind head)	Curl	Upright Rowing	Standing Press	Bench Press	(Squat) Deep Knee Bend	Bent Over Rowing	Back Raise	Standard Score	Percentile
70	112.5	125	165	175	265	150	220	100	100
65	110	122.5	160	170	255	145	215	95	99.9
62.5	107.5	120	155	165	245	142.5	210	90	99.8
60	105	117.5	150	160	235	140	205	85	99.4
57.5	102.5	115	145	155	230	135	200	80	98.4
55	100	112.5	140	150	220	130	195	75	96.2
52.5	97.5	110	135	145	210	125	190	70	90.3
50	95	107.5	130	140	200	120	185	65	84.2
45	90	105	125	135	190	117.5	180	60	75.8
42.5	87.5	100	120	130	180	115	175	55	64.0
40	85	95	115	125	170	110	170	50	50.0
37.5	82.5	92.5	110	120	160	105	165	45	36.0
35	80	90	105	115	150	102.5	160	40	24.2
30	75	85	100	110	140	100	155	35	15.8
27.5	72.5	80	95	105	130	95	150	30	9.7
25	70	77.5	90	100	120	90	145	25	3.8
22.5	67.5	75	85	95	110	85	140	20	1.6
20	65	72.5	80	90	105	80	135	15	.6
17.5	60	70	75	85	95	75	130	10	.2
15	57.5	67.5	70	80	85	70	125	5	.1
12.5	55	65	65	75	80	65	120	0	0

BODYWEIGHT CLASS 140–149 lbs.
1-RM

Sit-up (weight behind head)	Curl	Upright Rowing	Standing Press	Bench Press	(Squat) Deep Knee Bend	Bent Over Rowing	Back Raise	Standard Score	Percentile
70	117.5	130	170	185	275	205	225	100	100
65	115	127.5	165	180	270	197.5	220	95	99.9
62.5	112.5	125	160	175	260	190	215	90	99.8
60	110	122.5	155	170	250	180	210	85	99.4
57.5	107.5	120	150	165	240	175	205	80	98.4
55	105	117.5	145	160	230	167.5	200	75	96.2
52.5	102.5	115	140	155	220	160	195	70	90.3
50	100	112.5	135	150	210	150	190	65	84.2
45	95	110	130	145	200	145	185	60	75.8
42.5	92.5	107.5	125	140	190	137.5	180	55	64.0
40	90	105	120	135	180	130	175	50	50.0
37.5	87.5	102.5	115	130	170	122.5	170	45	36.0
35	85	100	110	125	160	115	165	40	24.2
30	82.5	95	105	120	150	110	160	35	15.8
27.5	80	90	100	115	140	100	155	30	9.7
25	77.5	87.5	95	110	130	95	150	25	3.8
22.5	75	85	90	105	120	90	145	20	1.6
20	72.5	82.5	85	100	115	85	140	15	.6
17.5	70	80	80	95	105	80	135	10	.2
15	67.5	77.5	75	90	100	75	130	5	.1
12.5	65	75	70	85	95	70	125	0	0

BODYWEIGHT CLASS 150–159 lbs.
1-RM

Sit-up (weight behind head)	Curl	Upright Rowing	Standing Press	Bench Press	(Squat) Deep Knee Bend	Bent Over Rowing	Back Raise	Standard Score	Percentile
75	122.5	135	175	195	290	210	230	100	100
72.5	120	132.5	170	190	285	202.5	225	95	99.9
70	117.5	130	165	185	275	195	220	90	99.8
65	115	127.5	160	180	265	185	215	85	99.4
62.5	112.5	125	155	175	255	180	210	80	98.4
60	110	122.5	150	170	245	172.5	205	75	96.2
57.5	107.5	120	145	165	235	165	200	70	90.3
55	105	117.5	140	160	225	155	195	65	84.2
50	100	115	135	155	215	150	190	60	75.8
47.5	97.5	112.5	130	150	205	142.5	185	55	64.0
45	95	110	125	145	195	135	180	50	50.0
42.5	92.5	107.5	120	140	185	127.5	175	45	36.0
40	90	105	115	135	175	120	170	40	24.2
35	85	102.5	110	130	165	115	165	35	15.8
32.5	82.5	100	105	125	155	105	160	30	9.7
30	80	97.5	100	120	145	100	155	25	3.8
27.5	77.5	95	95	115	135	95	150	20	1.6
25	75	92.5	90	110	125	90	145	15	.6
20	72.5	90	85	105	120	85	140	10	.2
17.5	70	87.5	80	100	115	80	135	5	.1
15	67.5	85	75	95	110	75	130	0	0

BODYWEIGHT CLASS 160–169 lbs.
1-RM

Sit-up (weight behind head)	Curl	Upright Rowing	Standing Press	Bench Press	(Squat) Deep Knee Bend	Bent Over Rowing	Back Raise	Standard Score	Percentile
75	125	140	180	205	305	215	235	100	100
72.5	122.5	137.5	175	200	300	207.5	230	95	99.9
70	120	135	170	195	290	200	225	90	99.8
65	117.5	132.5	165	190	280	190	220	85	99.4
62.5	115	130	160	185	270	185	215	80	98.4
60	112.5	127.5	155	180	260	177.5	210	75	96.2
57.5	110	125	150	175	250	170	205	70	90.3
55	107.5	122.5	145	170	240	160	200	65	84.2
50	105	120	140	165	230	155	195	60	75.8
47.5	102.5	117.5	135	160	220	147.5	190	55	64.0
45	100	115	130	155	210	140	185	50	50.0
42.5	97.5	112.5	125	150	200	132.5	180	45	36.0
40	95	110	120	145	190	125	175	40	24.2
35	92.5	107.5	115	140	180	120	170	35	15.8
32.5	90	105	110	135	170	110	165	30	9.7
30	87.5	102.5	105	130	160	105	160	25	3.8
27.5	85	100	100	125	150	100	155	20	1.6
25	82.5	97.5	95	120	140	95	150	15	.6
20	80	95	90	115	135	90	145	10	.2
17.5	77.5	92.5	85	110	130	85	140	5	.1
15	75	90	80	105	125	80	135	0	0

BODYWEIGHT CLASS 170–179 lbs.
1-RM

Sit-up (weight behind head)	Curl	Upright Rowing	Standing Press	Bench Press	(Squat) Deep Knee Bend	Bent Over Rowing	Back Raise	Standard Score	Percentile
75	124	145	185	215	315	220	240	100	100
72.5	122.5	142.5	180	210	310	212.5	235	95	99.9
70	120	140	175	205	300	205	230	90	99.8
65	117.5	137.5	170	200	290	195	225	85	99.4
62.5	115	135	165	195	280	190	220	80	98.4
60	112.5	132.5	160	190	270	182.5	215	75	96.2
57.5	110	130	155	185	260	175	210	70	90.3
55	107.5	127.5	150	180	250	165	205	65	84.2
50	105	125	145	175	240	160	200	60	75.8
47.5	102.5	122.5	140	170	235	152.5	195	55	64.0
45	100	120	135	165	225	145	190	50	50.0
42.5	97.5	117.5	130	160	215	137.5	185	45	36.0
40	95	115	125	155	205	130	180	40	24.2
35	92.5	112.5	120	150	195	125	175	35	15.8
32.5	90	110	115	145	185	115	170	30	9.7
30	87.5	107.5	110	140	175	110	165	25	3.8
27.5	85	105	105	135	165	105	160	20	1.6
25	82.5	102.5	100	130	155	100	155	15	.6
20	80	100	95	125	150	95	150	10	.2
17.5	77.5	97.5	90	120	145	90	140	5	.1
15	75	95	85	115	140	85	135	5	0

BODYWEIGHT CLASS 180–189
1-RM

Sit-up (weight behind head)	Curl	Upright Rowing	Standing Press	Bench Press	(Squat) Deep Knee Bend	Bent Over Rowing	Back Raise	Standard Score	Percentile
75	130	150	190	225	325	225	245	100	100
72.5	127.5	147.5	185	220	320	217.5	240	95	99.9
70	125	145	180	215	310	210	235	90	99.8
65	122.5	142.5	175	210	305	200	230	85	99.4
62.5	120	140	170	205	295	195	225	80	98.4
60	117.5	137.5	165	200	285	187.5	220	75	96.2
57.5	115	135	160	195	275	180	215	70	90.3
55	112.5	132.5	155	190	265	170	210	65	84.2
50	110	130	150	185	255	165	205	60	75.8
47.5	107.5	127.5	145	180	250	157.5	200	55	64.0
45	105	125	140	175	240	150	195	50	50.0
42.5	102.5	122.5	135	170	230	142.5	190	45	36.0
40	100	120	130	165	220	135	185	40	24.2
35	97.5	117.5	125	160	210	130	180	35	15.8
32.5	95	115	120	155	200	120	175	30	9.7
30	92.5	112.5	115	150	190	115	170	25	3.8
27.5	90	110	110	145	180	110	165	20	1.6
25	87.5	107.5	105	140	170	105	160	15	.6
20	85	105	100	135	165	100	155	10	.2
17.5	82.5	102.5	95	130	155	95	150	5	.1
15	80	100	90	125	150	90	145	0	0

BODYWEIGHT CLASS 190 lbs. +
1-RM

Sit-up (weight behind head)	Curl	Upright Rowing	Standing Press	Bench Press	(Squat) Deep Knee Bend	Bent Over Rowing	Back Raise	Standard Score	Percentile
75	135	155	195	235	335	230	250	100	100
72.5	132.5	152.5	190	230	330	222.5	245	95	99.9
70	130	150	185	225	320	215	240	90	99.8
65	127.5	147.5	180	220	315	205	235	85	99.4
62.5	125	145	175	215	305	200	230	80	98.4
60	122.5	142.5	170	210	295	192.5	225	75	96.2
57.5	120	140	165	205	285	180	220	70	90.3
55	117.5	137.5	160	200	275	175	215	65	84.2
50	115	135	155	195	265	170	210	60	75.8
47.5	112.5	132.5	150	190	260	162.5	205	55	64.0
45	110	130	145	185	250	155	200	50	50.0
42.5	107.5	127.5	140	180	240	147.5	195	45	38.0
40	105	125	135	175	230	140	190	40	24.2
35	102.5	122.5	130	170	220	135	185	35	15.8
32.5	100	120	125	165	210	125	180	30	9.7
30	97.5	117.5	120	160	200	120	175	25	3.8
27.5	95	115	115	155	190	115	170	20	1.6
25	92.5	112.5	110	150	180	110	165	15	.6
20	90	110	105	145	175	105	160	10	.2
17.5	87.5	107.5	100	140	165	100	155	5	.1
15	85	105	95	135	155	95	150	0	0

Table 7.9. Weight Training Measurement Chart

Body Area or Measurement	Date Measurement Taken						
Weight							
Neck							
Chest/Bust							
Upper Arm							
Forearm							
Waist							
Abdomen							
Hips							
Thigh							
Calf							
Ankle							
Harvard Step Test							
Vertical Jump							
Hand Grip							
Push-ups							
Percent Body Fat							

1-RM's

1. Sit-up	lbs.	Percentile	lbs.	Percentile
2. Curl	lbs.	Percentile	lbs.	Percentile
3. Upright row	lbs.	Percentile	lbs.	Percentile
4. Standing press	lbs.	Percentile	lbs.	Percentile
5. Bench press	lbs.	Percentile	lbs.	Percentile
6. Full squat	lbs.	Percentile	lbs.	Percentile
7. Bent row	lbs.	Percentile	lbs.	Percentile
8. Back raise	lbs.	Percentile	lbs.	Percentile

Specialized test results: If special tests were used to determine proficiency at a particular sport or skill, or if overall motor ability or fitness tests were taken, describe the results of the pre- and postsemester tests here.

Table 7.10. Weekly Log of Workouts

Name: Class   Date:

System of training:

EXERCISES	FIRST DAY				SECOND DAY				THIRD DAY		
(in sequence)	Sets	Reps.	Wt.		Sets	Reps.	Wt.		Sets	Reps.	Wt.

Table 7.10—*Continued*

*Comments:

Routine changes made this week:

---

*Note: Include all events which have impinged upon your workout schedule (i.e., how you feel, late getting to bed, better lifting technique, medications, etc.). This will assist you in assessing your progress more accurately.

Table 7.11. Workout Regimen with Sample Exercises

Sample Exercises	Pre-Test (1–RM)	1	2	3	4	5	6	7	8	9	10	Post Test (1–RM)	Percent Gain (1–RM)
Chest & Back													
Bench Press													
Upright Rows													
Incline Press													
Incline Flys													
Military Press													
Arms													
E–Z Curls													
Tricep Extension													
Alternate Dumbbell Curls													
French Press													
Wrist Curls													
Shoulders													
Dips													
Incline Press													
Front Pulldowns													
Pullovers													
Front Raises													

Legs
Leg Press

Half Squats

Leg Extension

Leg Curls

Toe Raises

Abdominals
Bent Leg Sit-ups

Crunchers

Twisted Sit-ups

Hyperextension

Leg Raises

Twist or Sidebends

Power Series
Full Squats

Power Cleans

Dead Lifts

Bench Press

Inclined Press

GLOSSARY/UNITS OF MEASURE

Glossary

A-Band: The dark striations of the myofibril.

Actin: Thin protein filament of the muscle which combines with the myosin cross-bridge to produce shortening tension.

Action Potential: Change in electrical activity across a nerve or muscle membrane.

Actomyosin: Refers to the interaction of actin and myosin protein filaments during muscle contraction.

Acute: Severe or short duration bout of exercise.

Adenosine Diphosphate (ADP): Chemical compound found in all cells resulting from the breakdown of ATP for energy during muscle contraction.

Adenosine Triphosphate (ATP): Chemical compound split into ADP and phosphate to produce energy.

Adipose Tissue: Tissue characterized by large fat storage.

Aerobic: Refers to the utilization of oxygen.

Aerobic Power: Physiological index expression of total body endurance, same as maximal oxygen uptake, maximal oxygen consumption, cardiovascular endurance capacity.

Afferent Nerve: Sensory nerve that conducts impulses from the senses to the central nervous system.

Alactacid Oxygen Debt: Oxygen used to restore ATP and PC in muscles during recovery.

All-or-None Law: Refers to a motor unit that either fires or does not fire.

Amino Acids: Nitrogen-containing substances that are the basic structures of proteins.

Amphetamines: Drugs that are synthesized to produce central nervous system stimulation similar to epinephrine.

Anabolic-Androgenic Steroids: Group of synthetic drugs having an effect on the body to produce male characteristics.

Anabolic Steroid: Drugs that are synthesized to produce the anabolic or growth-stimulating characteristics of the male androgen, testosterone.

Anaerobic: Refers to the absence of oxygen.

Anaerobic Threshold: Situation where metabolic demands of exercise cannot be covered comfortably by aerobic sources and anaerobic metabolism increases.

Androgenic Hormones: Hormones that affect and increase male sex characteristics.

Androgens: Steroid hormones that affect the male sex characteristics.

Anemia: Low count of red blood cells which limits oxygen transport or reduced hemoglobin concentration.

Angina Pectoris: Symptom usually associated with coronary heart disease (atherosclerosis) causing a strangling type pain in the chest area.

Arteriole: Small artery that controls the flow of blood from the arteries to the tiny capillaries.

Arteriosclerosis: Thickening and hardening of the arteries. An advanced stage of atherosclerosis or fatty build up on inner arterial wall.

Artery: An elastic vessel which carries blood from the heart.

Aspartates: Potassium and magnesium salts of the amino acid called aspartic acid.

ATP-PC System: Anaerobic energy system which provides the quickest source of ATP for use by muscles when PC is broken down to manufacture ATP.

Axons: Fiber extension from the nerve cell which conducts nerve impulses away from the nerve cell body.

Bar: There are two types of bars, the Olympic bar and the exercise bar. A variation of the Olympic bar is the power bar, used in powerlifting competition. Each bar is seven feet long and has revolving ends for easy handling of heavy weights. The power bar is slightly thicker than the Olympic bar due to the greater weight used by powerlifters. Exercise bars are typically five or six feet long, and are one inch in diameter the entire length to accommodate plates that have one inch holes. The Olympic bar ends are two inches in diameter. See E-Z Curl Bar.

Basal Metabolic Rate (BMR): Refers to the minimal muscle activity and other basic functions necessary for life of an organism.

Belts: Belts are used to support the lumbar spine during overhead lifting movements or heavy squatting and lifting from the floor. The spine hyperextends during overhead movements, whereas it flexes during squatting or pulling from the floor. Both movements can be dangerous to vertebral integrity if heavy weights are involved, but no belt should be worn when the weights are relatively light. This is so the tissues being stressed can get a chance to develop properly. Wear the belt to prevent injury from heavy weights, but allow lighter levels of stress to do the job of forcing some tissue adaptation by not wearing a belt.

Biopsy: Process involving the removal and examination of body tissues.

Blood Doping: Injection of either whole blood or packed red blood cells into a participant the day prior to competition in hopes of increasing blood volume and its oxygen-carrying capacity, thus improving endurance performance.

Blood Pressure: The force that blood exerts against the walls of the blood vessels and that makes the blood flow through the circulatory system.

Body Density: Mass per unit volume determined by dividing body weight measured in the air by the weight of the water displaced.

Bradycardia: Decreased or slower heart rate.

Buffer: Any compound that lessens the change in pH of a fluid when acids or bases are added.

Calorie: Refers to the amount of heat required to raise the temperature of water 1 degree centigrade.

Capillary: Network of small blood vessels located between arteries and veins where exchange of nutrients and gases between blood and tissues take place.

Carbohydrate: Basic foodstuff composed of hydrogen, oxygen, and carbon which makes up sugars, starches, and cellulose. Glucose, glycogen, fiber, and various saccharides are carbohydrates.

Carbohydrate Loading: Diet becomes predominantly carbohydrates three to four days prior to competition.

Cardiac Output: Refers to the amount of blood pumped by the heart in one minute; product of heart rate and stroke volume.

Cardiorespiratory Endurance: Ability of body to take in and distribute adequate amounts of oxygen to working muscles during physical activities.

Cardiovascular: Relating to the heart and blood vessels.

Central Nervous System: The brain and spinal chord.

Cerebellum: Part of brain located near the base of the skull which controls movement.

Cerebral Cortex: Grey matter of the brain which makes up the outer layer of the cerebrum.

Cerebum: Largest part of the brain composed of right and left hemispheres.

Cheating: The practice of swinging a weight through a sticking point so that heavier weights can be used. While not recommended for beginners, cheat movements can be effective in promoting development of strength and size if done properly. The weight should not be swung through the entire movement, but only through the sticking point.

Cholesterol: Fat like chemical found in all animal tissues.

Chronic: Refers to lasting a long time, even after the immediate stimulus has stopped.

Circuit Training: A routine of systematically selected exercises or activities that are performed in sequence at individual stations.

Clean and Jerk: One of the "Olympic" lifts.

Collagen: Fibrous protein that makes up a large part of ligaments and tendons.

Collars: Collars are used both inside and outside the plates to prevent them from slipping off the bar during use. There are many variations of collars, ranging from—½# clip collars to 5# Olympic collars.

Concentric Contraction: Shortening of muscle due to muscle contraction.

Cool-Down Period: The tapering off period after completion of the main conditioning bout. Activities such as slow jogging, walking, and static stretching are recommended.

Core Temperature: Body temperature monitored by the hypothalamus and insulated from environmental temperature.

Coronary Arteries: Blood vessels that carry blood away from the heart.

Cross-Bridges: Myosin extensions.

Cross Education: Training of the muscles of one limb causes a significant improvement in the opposite limb.

Cycle Training: Also known as "Periodization" referring to year-round training and long range planning.

Dead Lift: One of three power lifts.

Dehydration: Excessive loss of body water.

Dendrites: Cell body projections which pick up impulse and transmit toward the cell body.

Diastolic Pressure: Minimum level arterial blood pressure falls in the time between successive heart beats.

Diffusion: Movement of molecules due to their kinetic energy.

Disaccharide: Compound made up of two simple sugars.

Diuretics: Drugs that increase the output of salt and water in the urine (water pills such as chlorothiazide and spironlactone). Commonly used for treatment of hypertension.

Dynamic Contraction: Alternation of contracting and relaxing muscles.

Dysmenorrhea: Painful menstruation.

E-Z Curl Bar: A curling bar that is shaped to better emphasize the isolation of the biceps.

Eccentric Contraction: During contraction the muscle lengthens.

Ectomorphy: Body type having characteristics of linearity and fragility.

Efferent Nerve: Nerve cell that carries motor impulses away from the central nervous system to a response organ.

Electrocardiogram (EKG, ECG): Recording on graph paper showing the spread of the cardiac impulse through the heart.

Endomorphy: Body type having characteristics of roundness and softness.

Enzyme: Protein compound that speeds up a chemical reaction.

Epimysium: Sheath of connective tissue which holds the muscle fibers in bundles.

Epinephrine: Hormone produced by the adrenal gland which stimulates body structures that are not innervated by direct sympathetic fibers.

Ergogenic Aid: Factor that improves work performance.

Ergometer: A stationary exercise bicycle that can be adjusted to provide an accurate measurement of the work performed.

Estrogen: Female sex hormone responsible for growth of sex organs and secondary sex characteristics as well as cellular proliferation.

Evaporation: Loss of heat due to the conversion of water in sweat to a vapor.

Exercise Prescription: Individualizing the exercise workout based on intensity, duration, frequency, and mode of exercise as well as the individual fitness level of the participant.

Extrafusal Fiber: Normal muscle cell.

Fast-Twitch Fibers: Muscle fibers with fast contractile characteristics and a low capacity to use oxygen that are used in short duration activity.

Fat: A food substance used as a source of energy in the body and capable of being stored.

Fat-Free Weight: Your body weight free of fat (often referred to as lean body weight).

Fatigue: State of decreased capacity for work due to previous work load.

Fat-Soluble Vitamins: Vitamins soluble in solution only when attached to fatty acids.

Forced Reps: The practice of getting a partner to assist you in lifting the weight during the final two or three reps in a set so as to force additional adaptive growth from the muscle being exercised. Used primarily by advanced bodybuilders.

Functional Isometric Training: 1-RM held against fixed position for a short duration.

Glucose: The end product of carbohydrate that is transported in the blood (blood sugar) and metabolized in the cell. A monosaccharide; a thick, sweet, syrupy liquid.

Glycerol: Compound composed of three atoms of carbon combined with three hydroxyl groups that combines with fatty acids to form fat.

Glycogen: Common storage form of carbohydrate in muscle and liver.

Glycolysis: Metabolic breakdown of glycogen.

Golgi Tendon Organ: Proprioceptor found within a muscle tendon.

Hand Off: The act of assisting someone in getting a poundage in the proper lifting position before beginning the exercise.

Heat Cramp: Severe pain due to muscular contractions caused by prolonged exposure to environmental heat.

Heat Exhaustion: Extreme fatigue due to prolonged exposure to environmental heat.

Heat Stroke: Serious heat disorder due to overexposure to heat causing high temperature, dry skin, delirium, or unconsciousness, and sometimes death.

Hemoglobin: Protein of the red blood cell containing iron and capable of combining with oxygen.

Homeostasis: Striving of the body to maintain physiological stability.

Hormone: Chemical substance secreted by endocrine glands into the blood stream to effect other tissues or organs.

Hypertension: A higher than normal blood pressure, usually defined as any systolic pressure above 140 mmHg and a diastolic pressure in excess of 90 mmHg.

Hyperthermia: Increased body temperature.

Hypertrophy: The term used to describe the increase in size or mass of a cell, tissue, or organ (e.g., increase in muscle fiber size resulting from strength training).

Hyperventilation: Increased depth and frequency of breathing resulting in elimination of carbon dioxide.

Hypotension: Decreased blood pressure.

Hypoxia: Deficiency of oxygen in the blood or tissues.

Inspiratory Capacity: Maximum amount of air inspired from a resting expiratory level.

Intensity: The physiological stress on the body during exercise. Your level of intensity can be readily determined by measuring your pulse rate (heart rate) immediately following an exercise bout.

Intercostal Muscle: Muscles found between the ribs.

Interval Training: Successive bouts of exercise at near-maximal intensity, alternated with lighter periods of rest or exercise such as brisk walking or static stretching.

Intrafusal Fibers: Muscle fibers found within the muscle spindles.

Ischemia: Lack of blood flow (thus oxygen) to parts of the body.

Isokinetic Contraction: Muscular contraction in which a muscle puts force against a variable resistance.

Isometric (Static) Contraction: Muscular contraction in which a muscle creates force with no observable movement.

Isotonic Contraction: Muscular contraction in which a muscle creates force against a constant resistance causing either shortening or lengthening movement.

Kilocalorie (Kcal): Amount of heat required to raise the temperature of one kilogram of water one degree centigrade.

Kilopond Meter (kpm): Amount of force required to accelerate a mass of one kilogram one meter per second.

Kinesthesis: Body position awareness.

Krebs Cycle: Enzyme-catalyzed reactions in the mitochondria of cells which causes catabolism of fats, carbohydrates, and proteins to carbon dixoide and water.

Lactacid Oxygen Debt: Part of the recovery oxygen used to remove accumulated lactic acid from the blood following exercise.

Lactic Acid (Lactate): Final product of anaerobic glycolysis.

Lean Body Weight: The body weight minus the percent of body weight that is stored fat.

Lipid: A fat, or fatlike substance such as fatty acids, triglycerides and cholesterol.

Lipoprotein: A type of protein that carries cholesterol and triglycerides in the bloodstream.

Lock-Out: The last portion of any exercise movement resulting in straightened arms or legs or torso, completing the exercise.

Maximal Oxygen Uptake (Maximal Oxygen Consumption; Maximal Oxygen Intake; Maximal Aerobic Power; Max$\dot{V}O_2$): Maximum amount of oxygen that can be consumed per minute.

Menstruation: The periodic cycle in the uterus of the female associated with preparation of the uterus to receive a fertilized egg.

Mesomorphy: Body type characterized by square, hard, rugged, and prominent muscles.

Metabolism: Total of all the chemical changes in the body that make it possible for cellular function.

METS (Metabolic Equivalents): A measurement of energy expenditure (3.5 ml/kg body weight/min.). One MET represents the net energy cost during rest; two METS corresponds to two times the resting value.

Minerals: Twenty-two metallic elements necessary for cell functioning.

Mitochondria: Structures found in cell cytoplasm that contains the respiratory enzyme systems responsible for ATP formation.

Monosaccharides: Final product of digestion in the form of six carbon atom sugars, glucose, fructose, galactose.

Monounsaturated: Fat molecule in which the carbon chain contains one double bond.

Motor Cortex or Motor Area: Area of cerebral cortex that controls the nerve impulses causing contractions of skeletal muscles.

Motor Endplate: Neuromuscular junction where the motor nerve ending makes contact with the muscular fiber.

Motor Neuron: Nerve cell which affects muscular contraction.

Motor Unit: Motor neuron and all the muscle fibers innervated by the motor unit.

Muscle Fiber: A structural unit of muscle, often referred to as muscle cell.

Muscle Spindle: Receptor found among the fibers of a skeletal muscle that is stimulated by changes in muscle tension

Muscular Endurance: The capacity of a muscle to exert a force repeatedly or to hold a fixed or static contraction over a period of time.

Myelinated Nerves: Nerves wrapped by myelin sheaths (Schwann cells) that conduct faster than non-myelinated nerves.

Myocardial Infarction: Heart attack or death of the heart muscle (myocardium) due to lack of oxygen.

Myocardium: Heart muscle.

Myofibril: Active subunit of muscle contraction that is a subdivision of the muscle fiber embedded in the sarcoplasm of a muscle fiber.

Myoglobin: Iron-containing protein responsible for oxygen transport and storage in muscles.

Myoneural (Neuromuscular) Junction: Union of a muscle and its nerve cell, also called motor end plate.

Myosin: Protein that forms the thick filament of the myofibril involved in muscular contraction.

Myosin ATPase: Name given to the part myosin plays in catalyzing the breakdown of ADP and ATP during muscular contraction.

Norm: A standard of achievement represented by the average achievement of a large group.

Nutrient: The basic substances of the body that are provided by the eating of foods.

Obesity: Excessive amount of body fat.

Olympic Lifts: Two highly technical lifts performed by specialists in Olympic weight lifting, consisting of the "Clean and Jerk" and the "Snatch."

One-Repetition Maximum (1–RM): The greatest amount of weight that can be lifted just one time.

Overload Principle: Loading a cell or tissue with more than the usual amount of stress.

Oxygen Debt: Volume of oxygen used during exercise recovery above what is consumed at rest in the same period.

Oxygen Deficit: Period during exercise when oxygen consumption is below what is needed to supply the ATP required for the exercise.

Oxygen System: Aerobic energy system that produces ATP when food is broken down and provides most of the energy needed for endurance activities.

Partial Repetitions: Exercising without moving the resistance through a full range of motion, not making a complete contraction or extension of the muscle being exercised.

pH: Notation used to indicate the power of the hydrogen ion by giving the degree of acidity or alkalinity of a solution using 7 as neutrality.

Perimysium: Connective tissue surrounding a muscle bundle or fasciculus.

Peripheral Nervous System: Portion of the nervous system outside the brain or spinal cord.

Phosopholyphids: Fat found in the body which plays an important role in blood clotting and maintaining the membrane structure of all cells.

Phosphagen: Chemical compounds which refer collectively to ATP and PC.

Phosphocreatine (PC): Compound stored in muscles whose breakdown aids in producing ATP.

Plates: Plates used with power and Olympic bars range in size from 1¼—2½—5—10—25—35—45—100 pounds (all competitive weight lifting and powerlifting events require the use of kilogram plates of 1¼—2½—5—10—15—20—45 kilogram increments). Exercise plates generally follow the same pound increments as Olympic plates. Exercise plates have one inch holes whereas Olympic plates have two inch holes.

Plyometrics: A form of exercise such as vertical depth jumping or running in place that is employed sometimes with the use of weight vests or ankle weights to supplement weight training.

Polyunsaturated: Fat molecule in which carbon chain contains two or more double bonds.

Power: The rate at which force can be produced or the product of force and velocity; sometimes referred to as the explosive ability to apply force.

Power Lifts: Three lifting movements consisting of the Squat, Bench Press and Dead Lift.

Precapillary Sphincter: Band of smooth muscle that controls the blood flow into the true capillaries.

Proprioceptors: Sensory receptors in muscles, joints, and tendons which send information concerning body position and movements.

Proteins: Compounds composed of chains of amino acids which make one of the basic food-stuffs.

Pulse: Arterial wall distention which travels as a wave down the arteries.

Pyruvate (Pyruvic Acid): End product of aerobic glycolysis.

Reaction Time: Amount of time required to react to a stimulus.

Red Blood Cells: Blood cells that carry hemoglobin and get oxygen from the lungs to the tissues.

Repetition Maximum (RM): Maximum load that can be lifted over a given number of repetitions.

Reps: Short for repetitions. One rep is one full movement of the weight, as in performing one curl or one press, etc.

Residual Volume (RV): Amount of air that remains in the lungs after the maximum expiration.

Sarcolemma: Membrane of the muscle cell.

Sarcomere: Distance between the functional contractile unit that extends from Z line to Z line.

Sarcoplasm: Protoplasm in the muscle cell.

Sarcoplasmic Reticulum: Endoplasmic reticulum in the muscle cells that deal with calcium release, protein synthesis, and glycogen metabolism.

Sarcotubular System: System composed of tubules that aid in transmission of the electrical signal and provides an activating substance for muscle contractile process.

Saturated Fats: A food source found in meat, milk, cheese, and butter.

Semipermeable Membrane: Membrane selectively permeable to some but not all substances.

Sensory Nerve: Nerve cells that send impulses from a receptor to the central nervous system.

Sets: A set is a group of repetitions of a given exercise. Sets can vary in length from a single repetition (as in contest lifting) to as many as forty or fifty reps, depending upon what type of weight training program employed. Strength sets are comprised of four or five sets of three to eight reps, whereas endurance sets generally involve twenty or more reps each.

Sino-Atrial Node (SA Node): Specialized muscle mass known as the "pacemaker" which initiates each heart beat.

Skeletal Muscle: Muscle that attaches to the skeletal system and causes body movement by a shortening or pulling action of muscle on its bony attachment.

Skinfold Caliper: An instrument used to measure selected thickness of fat folds that have been pinched up on the body.

Slow-Twitch Fibers: Muscle fibers with slow contractile characteristics and high oxidative capacity associated with endurance-type activities.

Sluicegates: Pre-capillary sphincters that usually increase in caliber during exercise and are often associated with the "second wind theory."

Smooth Muscle: Involuntary muscle found in the walls of almost every organ of the body.

Snatch: Highly technical "Olympic" lift in which the weight bar is raised from the floor above the head in one continuous movement.

Somatotype: Physical classification of the human body. See ectomorph, mesomorph and endomorph.

Sphygmomanometer: Instrument designed to measure indirectly the arterial blood pressure.

Spotter: One or more training partners assisting a lifter in getting the weight from and back onto a rack [or helping the lifter when failing during a lift.] Spotters are essential particularly in the squat and bench press movements because of the potential danger involved.

Starling's Law of the Heart: States the greater the initial length of the cardiac muscle fiber, the stronger the myocardium contraction.

Static Contraction: Muscle tension during contraction is sustained throughout a period of activity.

Steady State: State during which a physiological function remains at a constant value.

Steroid: Substance derived from the male hormone, testosterone which has musculinizing properties.

Sticking Point: The position(s) in a given exercise movement where either gravity is at its greatest effect, or one muscle group ceases to assist, and another must take over (as in the squat at about 30° of hip flexion).

Strength: Capacity of a muscle or muscle group to develop and exert force during contraction.

Stretch Receptors: Refers to the muscle spindle and tendon organ.

Stretch Reflex: Basic neural mechanism for maintenance of muscle tonus.

Stroke Volume: Volume of blood pumped by the left ventricle during one heart beat.

ST Segment: Refers to the repolarization of the ventricles after contraction.

Submaximal Exercise: Rate of exercise that is less than maximum and is expressed as a percentage of maximal rate of oxygen uptake.

Synapse: Point at which two neurons are connected.

Systole: Contractile phase of the cardiac cycle.

Systolic Pressure: Highest level of arterial blood pressure during the systolic ejection of blood from the ventricle.

Testosterone: Male sex hormone having masculinizing properties.

Tidal Volume (TV): Amount of air expired or inspired with each breath.

Total Lung Capacity (TLC): Amount of air in the lungs after maximal inspiration.

Training Effect: The term used to describe the many physiological changes that result from participation in regular, vigorous, muscular fitness activities.

Training (or Target) Heart Rate: A heart beat rate (or pulse rate) per minute during exercise that will produce significant cardiorespiratory benefits.

Triad: Structure formed where two portions of the sarcoplasmic reticulum come together with a transverse tubule. It carries the action potential into the myofibrils.

Triglycerides: Fat particles that are stored in the body. They provide the main means for fat to be transported in the blood. Recent evidence has revealed an association with atherosclerosis.

Tropomyosin: Protein in the muscle associated with muscular contraction by producing an inhibiting effect upon actin-myosin interaction.

Troponin: Protein in the muscle associated with muscle contraction by producing a calcium interaction that releases the inhibition of actin-myosin interaction.

T-Tubules: Sarcolemma tubular invaginations that form a transverse network throughout the muscle fiber.

Unsaturated Fats: A liquid type of fat found in peanut and olive oil.

Valsalva Maneuver: Making a forced expiratory effort against a closed glottis.

Vasoconstriction: Decrease in the diameter of a blood vessel usually resulting in a blood flow reduction.

Vasodilation (Vasodilatation): Increase in the diameter of a blood vessel usually resulting in a blood flow increase.

Vasomotor: Referring to vasoconstriction and vasodilation.

Vein: Vessel of the circulatory system that carries blood toward the heart.

Viscera: Internal organs of the body.

Vital Capacity (VC): Maximum amount of air forced to be expired after a maximal inspiration.

Vitamins: Organic substances vital to cellular and metabolic functioning.

Warm-Up: An integral portion of your workout that is geared to preparing your body for a more vigorous exercise bout. Generally, walking, static stretching of major muscle groups, and light exercise that stimulates the heart, lungs, and muscles moderately and progressively are engaged in during warm-up.

Water-Soluble Vitamins: Vitamins that are soluble in water.

Work: Product of the application of a force through a distance.

Wraps: Elasticized fabric, similar to ace bandages but heavier. They are used by some lifters to prevent injury to knee and wrist joints during heavy lifting. Wraps are not recommended for sets involving eight or more reps since the tissues of the joints need that stress to become stronger. But, when lifting a weight that can't be properly performed for more than five reps, wraps can become important to prevent destructive stress being placed on the joints.

Units of Measure

Work/Energy

1 kilocalorie (Kcal) = 3087 foot-pounds = 426.4 kilograms-meters* = 426.4 kilopond-meters** = 4186 joules = 3.9680 British Thermal Units (B.T.U.)

1 foot-pound = 0.13825 kilogram-meters = 0.00032389 kilocalories = 1.3558 joules

1 kilogram-meter = 1 kilopond-meter = 7.23 foot-pounds = 0.0023427 kilocalories = 9.8066 joules

1 MET = approximately 0.25 liters of oxygen = approximately 1.25 kilocalories

Power (Work/Time)

1 horsepower = 4.564 kilogram-meter/minute = 33,000 foot-pounds/minute = 10,694 kilocalories/minute = 550 foot-pounds/second = 746 watts = 75 kilopond-meters/minute

1 kilocalorie/minute = 51.457 foot-pounds/second = 3.9685 B.T.U. = 0.093557 horsepower = 69.767 watts = 426.78 kilopond-meters/minute = 426.4 kilogram-meter/minute = 3087 foot-pounds/minute

1 watt = 0.73756 foot-pounds/second = 0.001341 horsepower = 6.12 kilopond-meters/minute = 0.01433 kilocalories/minute = 1 joule/second = 3.41304 B.T.U./hour = 44.22 foot-pounds/minute

1 liter O_2 consumed/minute = 15,575 foot-pounds/minute = 2153 kilogram-meter/minute = 5.05 kilocalorie/minute

1 foot-pound/minute = 0.1383 kilogram-meter/minute = 0.00003 horsepower = 0.0226 watt

1 kilogram-meter/minute = 7.23 foot-pounds/minute = 0.00022 horsepower = 0.1635 watt

Weight

1 pound = 16 ounces = 454 grams = 0.454 kilogram

1 kilogram = 35.27 ounces = 1,000 grams = 2.2046 pounds

1 gram = 0.035 ounces = 0.0022 pounds = 0.001 kilogram = 100 centigrams = 1000 milligrams

Distances

1 inch = 2.54 centimeters = 25.4 millimeters = 0.0254 meters

1 kilometer = 1,000 meters = 0.62137 miles

1 meter = 100 centimeters = 1,000 millimeters = 39.37 inches = 3.28 feet = 1.09 yards

*A kilogram-meter is the distance through which 1 kilogram moves 1 meter.

**A kilopond is the force acting upon a mass of 1 kilogram at normal acceleration of gravity.

1 foot = 30.48 centimeters = 304.8 millimeters = 0.304 meters
1 mile = 5280 feet = 1760 yards = 1609.35 meters = 1.61 kilometers
1 centimeter = 0.3937 inch = .01 meter

Volume

1 liter = 1.0567 U.S. quarts = 1,000 milliliters (ml)
1 milliliter = 0.03381 fluid ounces (fl. oz.)
1 pint = 0.473 liter = 0.5 quart
1 quart = 0.946 liters = 2 pints
1 tsp. = 5 milliliters
1 tblsp. = 15 milliliters
1 fl. oz. = 30 milliliters
1 cup = .024 liters
1 gallon = 3.8 liters

Velocity

1 mile/hour = 88 feet/minute = 1.47 feet/second = 0.45 meters/second = 26.8 meters/minute = 1.61
kilometers/hour
1 kilometer/hour = 0.62137 miles/hour = 16.7 meters/minute = 0.28 meters/second = 0.91 feet/
second
1 feet/second = 0.3048 meters/second = 18.3 meters/minute = 1.1 kilometers/hour = 0.68 miles/
hour

Temperature

$°F = (9/5 \times °C) + 32$
$0°C = 32°F$
$100°C = 212°F$
$273°K = 32°F = 0°C$
$°C = (°F − 32) \times 5/9$

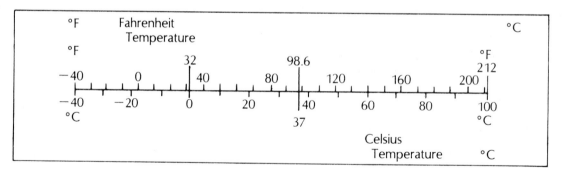

FORMULAS (Mechanics and Energy)

Mechanics
Coefficient of Friction: $\mu = \dfrac{F}{N}$
μ = coefficient of friction
F = force of friction   N = force normal to surface

Velocity: $V_{ot} = \dfrac{d}{t}$

V_{av} = average velocity
d = distance traveled t = elapsed time

Acceleration: $a = \dfrac{V_f - V_i}{t}$

a = acceleration V_i = initial velocity
V_f = final velocity t = elapsed time

Newton's 2nd Law of Motion: $F = m \cdot a$
F = force m = mass a = acceleration

Law of Universal Gravitation: $F = G\,\dfrac{m_1 \cdot m_2}{d^2}$

F = force of attraction $m_1 \cdot m_2$ = product of masses
G = gravitational constant d = distance between their centers

Centripetal Force: $F = \dfrac{m \cdot v^2}{t}$

F = centripetal force
m = mass v = velocity r = radius of path

Pendulum: $T = 2\pi \sqrt{\dfrac{l}{g}}$

T = period l = length g = acceleration of gravity

Work: $W = F \cdot d$
W = work F = force d = distance

Mechanical Advantage: $IMA = \dfrac{F_E \cdot d}{F_R \cdot d}$ $AMA = \dfrac{F_R}{F_E}$

IMA = ideal mechanical advantage AMA = actual mechanical
F_E = effort force   advantage
F_R = resistance force d = distance

Mechanical Equivalent of Heat: $W = J \cdot Q$
W = work J = mechanical equivalent of heat Q = heat

Energy
Kinetic Energy: $K.E. = \frac{1}{2} m \cdot v^2$

$K.E.$ = kinetic energy m = mass v = velocity

Potential Energy: $P.E. = m \cdot g \cdot h$

$P.E.$ = potential energy g = acceleration of gravity
m = mass h = vertical distance (height)

Relationship between Mass and Energy: $E = m \cdot c^2$

E = energy m = mass c = velocity of light

Selected Bibliography

American College of Sports Medicine. "Position Statement on the Use and Abuse of Anabolic-Androgenic Steroids in Sports," *Medicine and Science in Sports* 9 (1977):xi–xiii.

American Heart Association. *Exercise Testing and Training of Apparently Healthy Individuals: A Handbook for Physicians.* New York: American Heart Association, 1972.

Åstrand, P. O. and Rodahl, K. *Textbook of Work Physiology.* New York: McGraw-Hill, 1970.

Bentley, S. and Hatfield, F. C. *Women's Bodybuilding.* New Century Publishers, (In Press).

Berger, R. A. "Comparison Between Resistance Load and Strength Improvement." *Research Quarterly* 33 (1962):637.

Beyer, R. A. "Comparison of Static and Dynamic Strength Increase." *Research Quarterly* 33 (1962):329.

Chandler, J. V. "The Effects of Amphetamines on Selected Physiological Components Related to Athletic Success." *Medicine and Science in Sports* 10 (1978):38

Chui, E. F. "Effects of Isometric and Dynamic Weight Training Exercises Upon Strength and Speed of Movement." *Research Quarterly* 35 (1964):246.

Clarke, D. H. "Adaptations in Strength and Muscular Endurance Resulting from Exercise." In *Exercise and Sport Sciences Reviews.* Vol. 1, edited by J. H. Wilmore. New York: Academic Press, 1973.

Clarke, D. H. and Stull, G. A. "Endurance Training as a Determinant of Strength and Fatigueability." *Research Quarterly* 41 (1970):19–26.

Clarke, D.H. *Exercise Physiology.* Englewood Cliffs, New Jersey: Prentice-Hall, Inc., 1975.

Clarke, H. H. (ed.) "Muscular Power of the Legs." *Physical Fitness Research Digest* 8 (1978):1–24.

Clarkson, P. M., Kroll, W. and Melchionda, A. M. "Isokinetic Strength, Endurance and Fiber Type Composition of Elite American Paddlers." *European Journal of Applied Physiology and Occupational Physiology* 52 (1981):200–207.

Coleman, A. E. "Nautilus vs Universal Gym Strength Training in Adult Males." *American Corrective Therapy Journal* 31 (1977):103–107.

Costill, D. L., Dalsky, G. P., and Fink, W. J. "Effects of Caffeine Ingestion on Metabolism and Exercise Performance," *Medicine and Science in Sports* 10 (1978):155–158.

Costill, D. L. et al. "Skeletal Muscle Enzyme and Fiber Composition in Male and Female Track Athletes." *Journal of Applied Physiology* 40 (1976):149–154.

Councilman, J. "Isokinetic Exercise." *Athletic Journal.* February, 1972, 52, 6.

Delorme, T. L. and Watkins, A. L. "Techniques of Progressive Resistance Exercise." *Archives of Physical Medicine* 29 (1948):263.

deVries, H. A. *Physiology of Exercise.* Dubuque, Iowa: Wm. C. Brown Company Publishers, 1980.

Donald, K. W. et al. "Cardiovascular Responses to Sustained (Static) Contractions." *Circulatory Research* 20 (1967):1.

Enoka, R. M. "The Pull in Olympic Weightlifting." *Medicine and Science in Sports* 11 (1979):131–137.

Forsberg, A., Tesch, P. and Karlsson, J. "Effect of Prolonged Exercise on Muscle Strength Performance." *Biomechanics* 6–A (1978):62–67.

Gaines, C. and Butler, G. *Pumping Iron.* New York: Simon and Schuster, 1974.

Gettman, L. R., Pollock, M. L. and others. "Physiological Responses of Men to 1, 3, and 5 Day Per Week Training Programs." *Research Quarterly* 47 (1976):638–646.

Golding, L. A. et al. "Weight, Size and Strength Unchanged with Steroids." *The Physician and Sports Medicine* 2 (1974):39.

Gregory, L. W. "Some Observations on Strength Training and Assessment." *The Journal of Sports Medicine and Physical Fitness* 21 (1981):130–137.

Hatfield, F. C. "Getting the Most from Your Training Reps." *National Strength Coaches Association Journal* 4 (1982):28–29.

Hatfield, F. C. *Powerlifting: A Scientific Approach.* Contemporary Pub., 1981.

Hatfield, F. C. *The Science of Powerlifting,* Powerlifting USA: Camarillo, California, 1981.

Hatfield, F. C. and Krotee, M. L. "Weight Training for Pre-Adolescents." *Arena Review: The Institute for Sport and Social Analysis* 4 (1980):23–28.

Hatfield, F. C. *Weight Training for Young Athletes.* Atheneum Pub., 1980.

Hettinger, T. *Physiology of Strength.* Springfield, Ill.: Chas. C. Thomas, Pub., 1961.

Jaweed, J. M. et al. "Endurance and Strengthening Exercise Adaptations: Protein Changes in Skeletal Muscles." *Archives of Physical Medicine and Rehabilitation* 48 (1966):296.

Johnson, L. et al. "Anabolic Steroid: Effects on Strength, Body Weight, Oxygen Uptake and Spermatogenesis Upon Mature Males." *Medicine and Science in Sports* 4 (1972):43.

Johnson L. and O'Shea, J. P. "Anabolic Steroid: Effects on Strength Development." *Science* 164 (1969):957.

Johnson, W. R. and Buskirk, E. R. *Science of Medicine and Exercise in Sport.* New York: Harper and Row Publishers, 1974.

Karpovich, P. V. and Sinning, W. E. *Physiology of Muscular Activity.* 7th edition. Philadelphia: W. B. Saunders Co., 1971.

Katch, F. I. et al. "Estimation of Body Fat from Skinfolds and Surface Area." *Human Biology* 51 (1979):411–424.

Kiessling, K. H. et al. "Number and Size of Skeletal Muscle Mitochondria in Trained Sedentary Men." In *Coronary Heart Disease and Physical Fitness.* Edited by L. A. Larson and R. O. Malmbourg. Baltimore: University Park Press, 1971, p. 143.

Kroll, W. "Isometric Strength Fatigue Patterns in Female Subjects." *Research Quarterly* 42 (1971):286–288.

Krotee, M. L. "The Effect of Physical Activity on Various Psychosocial Constructs of University Students." *The Review of Sport and Leisure* 5 69–78, 1980.

Krotee, M. L. "The Physical Activity Program: Past and Future." *Journal of Physical Education and Recreation* 53 (1982):52–55.

Krotee, M. L., Alexander, J. F., Chein, I., LaPoint, J. D. and Brooks, H. "The Psychophysiological Characteristics of University Ice Hockey Players." In *Science in Skiing, Skating and Hockey.* Terauds, J. and Gros, H. J. (eds.), Delmar, California: Academic Publishers, 1979.

Krotee, M. L. and F. C. Hatfield. *The Theory and Practice of Physical Activity.* Dubuque, Iowa: Kendall/Hunt Publishing Company, 1979.

MacQueen, I. J. "Recent Advances in Techniques of Progressive Resistance Exercise." *British Medical Journal* 11(1954):1193.

Massey, B. H. et al. *Kinesiology of Weightlifting.* Dubuque: Wm. C. Brown Company Publishers, 1968.

McArdle, W. D. et al. *Exercise Physiology: Energy, Nutrition and Human Performance.* Philadelphia: Lea and Febiger, 1981.

McMorris, R. O., and Elkins, E. C. "A Study of Production and Evaluation of Muscular Hypertrophy." *Archives of Physical Medicine* 35(1951):420.

Morehouse, L. E. and Miller, A. T. *Physiology of Exercise.* St. Louis: C. V. Mosby Co., 1976.

Müller, E. A. "Influence of Training and Inactivity on Muscular Strength." *Archives of Physical Medicine and Rehabilitation* 41(1970):449.

Nichols, B. L. et al. "Syndrome Characterized by Loss of Muscle Strength Experienced by Athletes During Intensive Training Program." *Metabolism* 21 (1972):187.

Noble, L. "Effects of Resistance Exercise on Muscle Size, A Review." *American Corrective Therapy Journal* 24(1971):199.

O'Shea, J. P. *Scientific Principles and Methods of Strength Fitness.* Reading, Mass: Addison-Wesley Pub. Co., 1976.

———. "The Effects of an Anabolic Steroid on Dynamic Strength Levels of Weightlifters." *Nutritional Reports International* 4(1971):363.

Pearson, D. and Costill, D. "The Use of Anabolic Steroids of National Level Athletes." *National Strength Coaches Association Journal* 3 (1981):16–18.

Peterson, J. A. *Total Fitness: The Nautilus Way.* New York: Leisure Press, 1978.

Pipes, T. V. and Wilmore, J. H. "Isokinetic vs Isotonic Strength Training in Adult Men." *Medicine and Science in Sports* 7 (1975):262–274.

Pollock, M. L. et al. *Health and Fitness Through Physical Activity.* New York: John Wiley and Sons, 1978.

Pollock, M. L. et al. "Effect of Training Two Days Per Week at Different Intensities on Middle-aged Men." *Medical Science in Sports* 4(1972):192.

Rasch, P. J. and Burke, R. K. *Kinesiology and Applied Anatomy.* Philadelphia: Lea and Febiger, 1980.

Rogozkin, V. "Metabolic Effects of Anabolic Steroid on Skeletal Muscle," *Medicine and Science in Sports* 11 (1979):160–163.

Ryan, A. J. "Anabolic Steroids: The Myth Dies Hard." *The Physician and Sports Medicine.* (March, 1978):6, 3.

Saltin, B. et al. "Fiber Types and Metabolic Potentials of Skeletal Muscles in Sedentary Men and Endurance Runners." *Annals of the New York Academy of Science* 301 (1977):3.

Select Committee on Nutrition and Human Needs. *Dietary Goals for the United States.* United States Senate, December, 1977, U.S. Printing Office, Washington, D.C., 20402.

Shephard, R. J. "Intensity, Duration and Frequency of Exercise as Determinants of the Response to a Training Regime." *Int. Z. angew. Physiol.* 26(1968):272.

Sinclair, R. "Method of Comparing Weightlifters." *International Olympic Lifter* 4 (1977):20–21.

Spitler, D. L., Diaz, F. J., Horvath, S. M. and Wright, J. E. "Body Composition and Maximal Aerobic Capacity of Body Builders." *The Journal of Sports Medicine and Physical Fitness* 20 (1980):181–188.

Starr, R. *The Strongest Shall Survive.* Annapolis: Fitness Products, Ltd., 1976.

Terauds, J. *Science in Weightlifting.* Delmar, California: Academic Publishers, 1979.

Tesch, P. et al. "Muscle Fatigue and Its Relation to Lactate Accumulation and LDH Activity in Men." *Acta Physiologica Scandinavica* 103 (1978):413–420.

Thomas, V. *Science and Sport, How to Measure and Improve Athletic Performance.* Boston: Little, Brown and Co., 1970.

Ward, P. "The Effects of Anabolic Steroid on Strength and Lean Body Mass." *Medicine and Science in Sports* 5 (1973):277.

Weltman, A. and Katch, V. I. "A Nonpopulation-specific Method for Predicting Total Body Volume and Percent Fat." *Human Biology* 50 (1978):151–158.

Williams, M. H. *Nutrition for Fitness and Sport.* Dubuque, Iowa: Wm. C. Brown Publishers, 1983.

Williams, S. R. *Essentials of Nutrition and Diet Therapy.* St. Louis: C. V. Mosby Co., 1974.

Wilmore, J. H. *Training for Sport and Activity.* Boston: Allyn and Bacon, Inc., 1982.

Zinovieff, A. N. "Heavy Resistance Exercise, the Oxford Technique." *British Journal of Physical Medicine* 14 (1951):129.

Annotated Periodicals Concerning Weight Training

Health & Strength, monthly issue, from Health & Strength Publishing Co. Ltd., Halton House, 20–23 Holborn, London E. C. 1, UK.

> Covers all phases of weight training. Particularly strong on articles for women and news of the annual NABBA Mr. Universe contest. Edited by Oscar Heidenstam.

Iron Man, bimonthly issue, from Iron Man Publishing Company, 512 Black Hills Avenue, Alliance, Nebraska 69301.

> Excellent coverage of bodybuilding, weight lifting and powerlifting. Considered by the weight training elite to be the least biased of all American publications. Edited by Peary Rader.

Muscle & Fitness, monthly issues, from Muscle Builder Publications, Inc., 21100 Erwin Street, Woodland Hills, California 91364.

> Very heavy concentration on advanced bodybuilders. The Official IFBB periodical. Strong commercial bias in virtually all articles. Edited by Gene Mozee.

Muscle Mag International, quarterly issue (with plans to expand to monthly), from Health Culture, Subscription Department, 270 Rutherford Road South, Brampton, Ontario, Canada L6W 3K7.

> A new magazine on the scene concentrating on all phases of bodybuilding. The editorial policy is to present articles appealing to the general public more than to hard core bodybuilders. Edited by Robert Kennedy.

Muscle Training Illustrated, bi-monthly, from Muscle Man, Inc., 1664 Utica Avenue, Brooklyn, New York 11234.

> Caters almost exclusively to contest bodybuilders. Fairly strong commercial slant to most material. Edited by Dan Lurie.

Muscular Development, bi-monthly, from Muscular Development, P.O. Box 1707, York, Pennsylvania 17405.

> Covers powerlifting and bodybuilding, usually with several authoritative articles on each subject. Occasional commercial slant to articles. Edited by John C. Grimek.

National Strength & Conditioning Association Journal, 6 issues/year, from National Strength and Conditioning Association, P.O. Box 81410, Lincoln, Nebraska 68501.

> A fine resource for all forms of lifting and conditioning. Carries sport specific information. Edited by some of the best experts in the United States.

Powerman, bi-monthly issue, from Powerman Magazine, P.O. Box 3005, Erie, Pennsylvania 16508.

> Devoted exclusively to the sport of powerlifting. Plenty of photos, contest results, and training advice articles.

Strength & Health, bi-monthly, from Strength & Health, P.O. Box 1707, York, Pennsylvania 17405.

> Emphasis on Olympic style weight lifting and family fitness through weight training and proper nutrition. Carries women's articles and occasional profiles of famous athletes who train with weights.

Notes

Notes

Notes

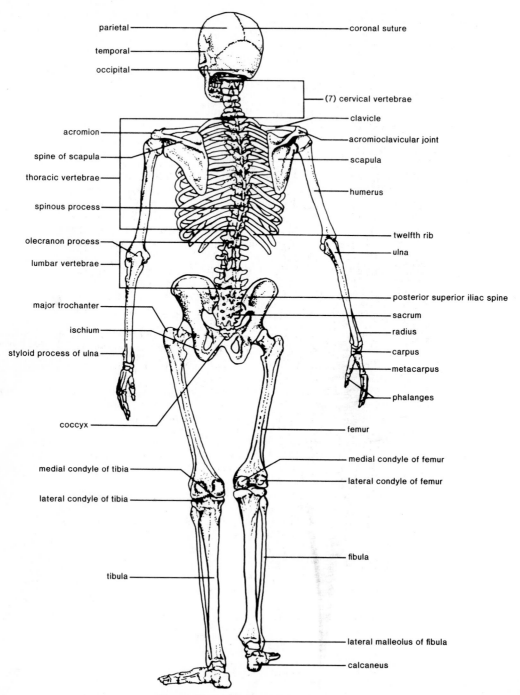

parietal —————— coronal suture

temporal ——————

occipital ——————

———— (7) cervical vertebrae

———— clavicle

acromion ——————

—————— acromioclavicular joint

spine of scapula ——————

—————— scapula

thoracic vertebrae ——————

—————— humerus

spinous process ——————

—————— twelfth rib

olecranon process ——————

—————— ulna

lumbar vertebrae ——————

—————— posterior superior iliac spine

major trochanter ——————

—————— sacrum

ischium ——————

—————— radius

styloid process of ulna ——————

—————— carpus

—————— metacarpus

—————— phalanges

coccyx ——————

—————— femur

—————— medial condyle of femur

medial condyle of tibia ——————

—————— lateral condyle of femur

lateral condyle of tibia ——————

—————— fibula

tibula ——————

—————— lateral malleolus of fibula

—————— calcaneus

Human Skeletal System, Posterior View